WHAT THINK YE
OF CHRIST?
And Other Sermons

WHAT THINK YE
OF CHRIST?
And Other Sermons

by
Oliver B. Greene

The Gospel Hour, Inc., Oliver B. Greene, Director
P. O. Box 2024, Greenville, South Carolina

First printing, July 1965—10,000 copies
Second printing, June 1967—10,000 copies
Third printing, December 1968—15,000 copies
Fourth printing, May 1970—15,000 copies
Fifth printing, November 1973—15,000 copies
Sixth printing, November 1974—15,000 copies

$4.00

CONTENTS

WHAT THINK YE OF CHRIST?

WHAT THINK YE OF CHRIST?

"While the Pharisees were gathered together, Jesus asked them, saying, What think ye of Christ? Whose Son is He?" (Matt. 22:41,42).

The way you answer this question will determine where you spend eternity—in heaven, or in hell!

The sin-question has been settled. Jesus settled it—once, for all, forever (Heb. 10:14). The sin-debt has been paid, redemption has been purchased, the ransom has been satisfied.

Jesus was God in flesh, reconciling the world unto Himself (II Cor. 5:19). Salvation has been brought down to man and presented in Christ Jesus; but unless you *think right* about Christ, you cannot be saved.

Personally, politically, socially, or religiously, Jesus is the supreme issue wherever and whenever He appears. To Thomas He said, "I am the Way, the Truth, the Life. No man cometh unto the Father but by me" (John 14:6).

When Jesus tabernacled among men here on earth, His appearance became the supreme center of human interest. He is called "the Prince of Peace," but He is also *the great Disturber*! Debate, discussion, controversy, and division follow His presence as surely as sunset follows the sunrise. To His disciples He said, "Think not that I am come to send peace on earth: I came not to send peace, but a sword. For I am come to set a man at variance against his father, and the daughter against her mother, and the daughter-in-law against her mother-in-law. And a man's foes shall be they of his own household" (Matt. 10:34–36).

Christ not only *makes* issues — but Himself, the Man

9

of men, IS the issue. When He appeared, whether in Galilee, Capernaum, or Jerusalem, men began to ask, "*Who IS this Man*?" When He opened the eyes of the blind, cleansed the leper — even when He raised the dead — *in spite* of the miracles and the evidence at hand, men asked, "By what *authority* does He do these things?"

In Jerusalem, the controversy about Him sometimes reached the boiling point. Opinion concerning Him ran the extremity of the scale, from the lowest to the highest. Some said that He was a man *demon-possessed*, while others confessed that He was *the Son of God*.

Today, opinion concerning Christ Jesus still runs the extremity of the scale. Some believe Him to have been an illegitimate impostor, but thank God *millions* believe that He was the beloved, only begotten Son of God!

Jesus On Trial

While men were asking, "Who is He?" and discussing whether He was an impostor or the Son of God, *Jesus* testified concerning Himself — and the claims He made were the most *extraordinary* (and if not true, the most *blasphemous*) claims ever made by man!

But to each of those claims He gave support. He said that His testimony was supported by the heavenly Father, He claimed to be *one with the Father*, and He supported that testimony in these words: "When ye have lifted up the Son of man, then shall ye know that I am He, and that I do nothing of myself; but as my Father hath taught me, I speak these things. And He that sent me is with me: the Father hath not left me alone; for I do always those things that please Him" (John 8:28,29).

Thus, every word He spoke and everything He did is established and proved "at the mouth of two witnesses"

10

as demanded by the Law (Deut. 17:6). He was not doing or speaking these things alone, but the Father taught Him and spoke through Him. Every miracle He performed, every wonder He displayed, the extraordinary wisdom He manifested and the tremendous force of His personality are all singular in that they testify to His being more than ordinary man. He was "a Man approved of God . . . by miracles and wonders and signs, which God did by Him" (Acts 2:22).

In dealing with the Pharisees, Jesus did not appeal simply to Himself, to His personality, His words, His miracles; nor did He appeal only to the manifest presence of God the Father in His miracle-working power. He took His enemies at a disadvantage by using their own star witness—the Word of God—and challenged them with these words:

"Search the Scriptures; for in them ye think ye have eternal life: and they are they which testify of me" (John 5:39). He knew that His bitterest enemies were students of the very Scriptures that prophesied *concerning* Him and pointed clearly to His coming. The law and the prophets gave witness to Him, the Scriptures furnish the undeniable measurements by which He is identified and by which He could have been *recognized* as He tabernacled among men. The Pharisees to whom He spoke were familiar with Isaiah 53, and with many other Scriptures concerning Christ in the law, the prophets, and Psalms. But even though they knew the Scriptures, they steadfastly refused to recognize the Saviour.

Those to whom Jesus spoke on that particular day have passed on, but there are many like them today. Men place much emphasis upon the Christ of experience. They compare Him with the Christ of Scripture, they *add* a little and *take away* a little, thus reducing Him to a great Man, a great Teacher, a great Healer, Founder of a great religion;

but He was more than these! *The Christ of the Scripture is the only begotten Son of God, virgin-born — very God in flesh,* equal with the Father in every respect.

By listening to religious leaders and theologians, you, too, might not know who this Man is; but if you believe the final authority of God concerning Him, you will find that the Scriptures clearly testify that Christ is the Son of God— holy, undefiled, without sin, *separate from sinners* and yet bearing the sin of the whole wide world in His body on the cross!

As you search the Scriptures, you will discover that Christ lived a supernatural life—a spiritual life, not carnal; and He calls upon US to live as HE lived. When we believe on Him and trust Him as Saviour, we are made partakers of His nature. We are transformed by the power of the Holy Spirit. We are born into God's family through the incorruptible seed, the Word of God, and we are predestined to be conformed to His likeness.

In the Gospel of John, beginning with chapter 5 and continuing through chapter 10, we have the record of certain controversies and discourses concerning the Lord Jesus Christ; and anyone who will read that portion of Scripture with an open mind, minus preconceived ideas and notions, forgetting *what MAN has said* about the Lord Jesus Christ, will be convinced that "Truly, this Man was the Son of God!" (Mark 15:39).

Whatever Jesus did during His earthly ministry—preaching, teaching, performing miracles, or making a journey— was for one primary purpose: *to declare Himself the Son of God, and present Himself as Saviour of sinners.* He never performed a miracle to bring comfort or gain to Himself.

"I Am the Bread of Life"

John 6:1—13 records Christ's miraculous feeding of

12

5,000 men (not counting women and children) with only five loaves and two fishes. The people were so impressed by this miracle that they determined to take Him by force and make Him a King, but "He departed again into a mountain Himself alone" (John 6:15).

When they found Him again the next day, they asked Him, "What shall we do, that we might work the works of God?" Jesus replied, "*This* is the work of God, that ye believe on Him whom He hath sent!" They were not willing to *believe* simply because He declared that He was the Son of God, and that He had proceeded from the Father.

They then asked Him, "What sign shewest thou then, that we may see, and believe thee? What dost thou work? Our fathers did eat manna in the desert; *as it is written*, He gave them bread from heaven to eat." Here they made known their knowledge of the Scriptures — but they had not found the Lord Jesus in them. He was there for them to find, had they searched in faith with an open heart.

Jesus then declared: "Verily, verily, I say unto you, Moses gave you not that bread from heaven; but my Father giveth you the true bread from heaven. For the bread of God is He which cometh down from heaven, and giveth life unto the world. Then said they unto Him, Lord, evermore give us this bread. And Jesus said unto them, I AM THE BREAD OF LIFE: he that cometh to me shall never hunger; and he that believeth on me shall never thirst" (John 6:22–35 in part).

These were the people who, only a day before, had seen Him feed the multitudes with the pitifully few loaves and fishes furnished by a little lad. Anyone present on that occasion should have known that no ordinary man could have performed such a miracle; and they were also aware that after He slipped away from them He had crossed

13

the sea in some supernatural way (John 6:15–25). Now He offered them eternal life on the basis of their faith in Him — and they rejected His offer! Instead, they demanded, "Show us a sign, that we may believe."

How could they have been so *blind*! They had not heard the message of His words, they had failed miserably in seeing the significance of His miracle of the loaves and fishes — and now they demanded *another* miracle. But Jesus had no time to waste. If they had not recognized Him in miracles past, would they recognize His supernatural power if He worked another miracle? He did not perform such wonders merely to satisfy the curiosity of unbelievers. Every detail of His life and stewardship was directed toward assuring men of His identity, and of His reason for coming into the world.

They not only demanded that He work a miracle, they suggested the TYPE of miracle He should perform! They pointed out that Moses had given manna to the fathers in the wilderness, suggesting that if HE were able to produce manna from the sky, they would believe on Him; but their suggestion went deeper than that. They were indicating that as disciples of Moses, they *believed Moses* and therefore did not need to hear the words of Jesus.

He accepted their challenge — and He used the miracle they suggested concerning Moses, by taking it out of the *physical* realm and putting it into the realm of the *spiritual*. He said, "Moses did NOT give you that bread. The manna which came down from heaven was God-given, and if you would learn the lesson God has for you, you must understand that the vast majority of your fathers who ate that manna revolted against God *in spite of* the manna, and God sent His wrath upon them in judgment."

God did not give the manna in the wilderness simply

14

to satisfy physical appetite. He was attempting to point them to the *spiritual Bread*, that they might live eternally.

Paul later affirmed that when the Hebrew fathers drank of the rock in the wilderness, they drank of Christ. He clearly says, *"That Rock was Christ."* The manna was given—not by Moses, but by God the Father; and as the water from the rock was Christ, so the manna pointed to the bread that God would send down from heaven—even the Lord Jesus Christ.

"The Jews then murmured at Him, because He said, I am the bread which came down from heaven. And they said, Is not this Jesus, the son of Joseph, whose father and mother we know? How is it then that He saith, I came down from heaven?" (John 6:41,42).

But Jesus said a second time, *"I am that Bread of Life. . .* Verily, verily, I say unto you, Except ye eat the flesh of the Son of man, and drink His blood, ye have no life in you. Whoso eateth my flesh, and drinketh my blood, hath eternal life; and I will raise him up at the last day. For my flesh is meat indeed, and my blood is drink indeed. He that eateth my flesh, and drinketh my blood, dwelleth in me, and I in him. As the living Father hath sent me, and I live by the Father: so he that eateth me, even he shall live by me. This is that Bread which came down from heaven: not as your fathers did eat manna, and are dead: he that eateth of this Bread shall live for ever" (John 6:48—58 in part).

When Jesus had finished this discourse, *"many of His disciples went back, and walked no more with Him."* Jesus then turned to the twelve, and asked, "Will ye also go away?" Simon Peter replied, "Lord, to whom shall we go? Thou hast *the words of eternal life.* And we believe and are sure that thou art that Christ, the Son of the living

God'' (John 6:67—69).

Jesus had said to His disciples, "The WORDS that I speak unto you, they are spirit, and they are life." Peter said, "Thou hast the WORDS of eternal life." We understand, then, what Jesus meant when He said, "*Except ye eat my flesh and drink my blood . . .*" for John tells us that "in the beginning was the WORD, and the WORD was with God, and the WORD was God. . . and the WORD was made flesh and dwelt among us."

What Jesus was saying was simply this: "Except ye receive my WORD, except you appropriate, assimilate, and take into your heart by faith, the WORDS that I speak, you cannot be saved, because the WORDS that I speak are spirit and they are life."

In John 5:24 He said, "Verily, verily, I say unto you, He that heareth my WORD, and believeth on Him that sent me, hath everlasting life, and shall not come into condemnation; but is passed from death unto life."

I Peter 1:23 tells us that we are born again, "not of corruptible seed, but of incorruptible, by the WORD of God, which liveth and abideth for ever."

In John 12:48 Jesus said, "He that rejecteth me, and receiveth not my WORDS, hath one that judgeth him: the WORD that I have spoken, the same shall judge him in the last day."

In His discourse on the bread of life, Jesus thrust Himself into the midst of the Old Testament Scriptures which the Jews had long searched and diligently studied; and IN those Scriptures He pointed out the significance of the testimony of God through the manna given to the children of Israel. He set forth the truth that He IS the Bread of life, He is the Life-Giver, *and only through HIM can men live eternally.*

16

"I Am the Light of the World"

"Then spake Jesus again unto them, saying, I am the Light of the world: He that followeth me shall not walk in darkness, but shall have the light of life. The Pharisees therefore said unto Him, Thou bearest record of thyself; *thy record is not true!*" (John 8:12,13).

Now what the Pharisees really said was this: "You are a *liar!* You are an impostor. You bear record of yourself, and your record is *not true!*"

Then Jesus turned again to the Scriptures, yea, to the law of Moses, in an attempt to show them that He WAS the Light of the world. He said, "Ye judge after the flesh; I judge no man. And yet if I judge, my judgment is true: for I am not alone, but I and the Father that sent me. *It is also written in your law*, that the testimony of two men is true. I am ONE that bear witness of myself, and the FATHER that sent me beareth witness of me" (John 8:15—18).

No doubt at least some of these Pharisees, scribes, and elders were present when Jesus was baptized, and they heard God's voice from heaven when He announced, "This is my beloved Son, in whom I am well pleased" (Matt. 3:17). Jesus declared that He was the Son of God, and GOD witnessed what the Son said. They had witnessed the miracle of the water turned to wine at the marriage in Cana, they were present at the feeding of the five thousand, they saw the miraculous healing of the man who had been paralyzed for 38 years — but they still refused to believe!

It was then that Jesus said to them, "When ye have lifted up the Son of man, *then shall ye know* that I am He." And we know that when Jesus was lifted up on the cross, God DID testify! Darkness covered the face of the earth, the veil in the temple was rent from top to bottom, graves were opened and the bodies of the saints came out of the

17

graves and walked the streets of Jerusalem!! Yes, when they crucified the Son of God, the Father gave testimony that they could not deny.

Jesus claimed nothing less than that He Himself was the standard of measurement, the scales, the test of character for all mankind. By HIM all men are measured, by His character all men are weighed. He is the Light that points to heaven, and those who ignore that Light will walk in darkness, and spend eternity in the blackness of darkness forever.

But the Jews repudiated this claim. They called Him a liar. They said they were disciples of Moses, descendants of Abraham. The Pharisees, scribes, elders and chief priests had laid their own foundation for their faith, and in their own eyes they were superior to others in the favor of God. They were proud, arrogant, self-righteous. When Jesus said, "Ye shall know the truth, and the truth shall make you free," they turned on Him in fury and cried out, "WE be Abraham's seed, and were never in bondage to any man! How sayest thou, Ye shall be made free?" (John 8:32,33).

If Jesus had reacted according to the religious customs of our day, He would have neatly sidestepped the issue and thereby would have avoided a conflict; but the Son of God did not believe in compromise, nor in "going along with the crowd." With firm insistence He pressed home His claims:

"If ye were Abraham's children, ye would do the works of Abraham. But now ye seek to kill me, a Man that hath told you the truth, which I have heard of God: this did not Abraham. . . Ye are of your father the devil, and the lusts of your father ye will do" (John 8:39—44 in part).

They knew Abraham, who was indeed a great man, the "friend of God." But One greater than Abraham was present

18

with them now. Abraham was only a man; JESUS was the God-man, the virgin-born Son of God. In the presence of Jesus, humanity can only humble itself and worship, for humanity cannot be compared with Deity.

Again the Jews forgot the miracles He had performed, they forgot the Voice from heaven announcing, "This is my beloved Son!" They asked Him, "Thou art not yet fifty years old, and hast thou seen Abraham?" Jesus replied, "Verily, verily, I say unto you, *Before Abraham was, I AM!*"

Then they took up stones to stone Him; but He hid Himself "and went out of the temple, going through the midst of them, and so passed by" (John 8:53—59 in part).

Jesus was born as no mortal was ever born, He lived as no mortal ever lived. He taught as no mortal ever taught. "Before Abraham was, I AM" could be said by Jesus, and be *pure truth*.

Years later, John the Beloved sums up the whole Gospel message by giving the apostolic testimony to his personal investigation of Jesus, and also by the other disciples:

"That which was from the beginning, which we have heard, which we have seen with our eyes, which we have looked upon, and our hands have handled, of the Word of life; (For the life was manifested, and we have seen it, and bear witness, and shew unto you that eternal life, which was with the Father, and was manifested unto us;) That which we have seen and heard declare we unto you that ye also may have fellowship with us: and truly our fellowship is with the Father, and with His Son Jesus Christ. And these things write we unto you, that your joy may be full. This then is the message which we have heard of Him, and declare unto you, that God is light, and in Him is no darkness at all. If we say that we have fellowship with Him, and walk in darkness, we lie, and do not the truth: But if we walk in the light, as He is in the light, we have fellowship one with another, and the blood of Jesus Christ His Son cleanseth us from all sin" (I John 1:1-7).

What John is saying is simply this: "That which we saw, that which we heard, that which we handled concerning Him, proved to us that He was God manifested in flesh."

And since they had seen Him, heard Him, touched Him, they declared, "This is the message which we received from Him ... *God is light, and in Him is no darkness at all!*"

The entrance of the Word gives light. Apart from hearing, believing, and receiving the Word, there IS no light, there is no eternal life. He who hears and believes the Word has everlasting life and shall not come into judgment, but is passed from the darkness of death into the kingdom of light—the kingdom of God's dear Son (Col. 1:13).

"I Am the Good Shepherd"

Jesus first said, "I am the Bread of life," offering to His people life through the living Bread. As the Bread of life, He *supplies* life.

He then said, "I am the Light of the world," offering to them the path of light that leads to life everlasting. As the Light of the world He provides light in which to walk.

And then, He said, "I am the good Shepherd," offering them liberty. As the Good Shepherd of the sheep, He leads into green pastures—and liberty! Those to whom He was speaking at that time were attempting to enter the kingdom by another way—by Judaism and the Law, claiming Moses as their prophet and Abraham as their forefather. But Jesus clearly said, "He that entereth not by the door into the sheepfold, but climbeth up some other way, the same is a thief and a robber. But he that entereth in by the door is the Shepherd of the sheep. . . I AM THE GOOD SHEPHERD: the good Shepherd giveth His life for the sheep'' (John 10:1,2,11).

The 23rd Psalm becomes the personal experience of every born again believer. To Israel, Jehovah was their Shepherd. They had searched the Scriptures, yet failed to see the Good Shepherd, the Lord Jesus Christ, who came to lay down His life for the sheep.

As Jesus spoke, probably every person present was familiar with the 23rd Psalm, the Psalm of David the shepherd boy. They knew the quotation, "The Lord is my Shepherd," but they refused to see in Jesus the Shepherd of the sheep. They refused to listen to His words as He attempted to lead them into green pastures beside still waters and restore their souls.

In John 10:30 Jesus declared, "I and my Father are one," and the Jews took up stones to stone Him. He then asked them, "Many good works have I shewed you from my Father; *for which of those works do ye stone me?*"

The Jews answered Him, "For a good work we stone thee not; but for blasphemy; and because that thou, being a man, makest thyself God."

Jesus then said, "Is it not written in your law, I said, Ye are gods? If He called them gods, unto whom the Word of God came, and the Scripture cannot be broken; say ye of Him, whom the Father hath sanctified, and sent into the world, Thou blasphemest; because I said, I am the Son of God? If I do not the works of my Father, believe me not. But if I do, though ye believe not me, believe the works: that ye may know, and believe, that the Father is in me, and I in Him."

The Jews then sought again to take Him, "but He

escaped out of their hand'' (John 10:30—39).

In His discussion with the Pharisees and scribes, Jesus used the testimony of three great Old Testament characters to prove Himself very God, and He declared Himself to be greater than any and all:

Concerning *Abraham*, father of the faithful and friend of God, He said, *"Before Abraham was, I AM."*

Concerning *Moses* the law-giver, He declared that the manna from heaven was given by God, and that HE was the living bread—*the Bread of Life*.

Concerning *David* the king, He declared Himself to be the King of David and pointed out that David had referred to Him as "my Shepherd."

Thus, Abraham, Moses, and David, three of the greatest men in Bible history, all yield their testimonies to Jesus the Messiah. In the book of Hebrews, a commentary on the Old Testament message, we find a definite declaration that the Lord Jesus Christ is greater than the angels, greater than Moses, greater than Joshua, greater than Aaron, greater than Melchisedec. Surely anyone who will search the Scriptures with an open mind and open heart must confess that this Man Christ Jesus was without a doubt the Son of Almighty God!

If there is any doubt in your heart, dear reader, as to whom the Lord Jesus is, *search the Scriptures* — "they are they which testify of HIM." Do not allow the devil to plant doubts in your mind or despair in your heart. The Word of God is quick and powerful and sharper than any twoedged sword — it is a lamp unto our feet, and it will enlighten, lead, convict, convince, and *convert* all who will read it, believe it, and receive it.

In the Lord Jesus Christ, and in HIM alone, there is

light, life, and liberty. You must know *Him* if you want to know life. To reject Him is to walk in darkness and spend eternity in the blackness of darkness forever.

Christ is before you; He is the supreme issue of your life. You *must* answer the question, "What think YE of Christ? Whose Son do YOU believe Him to be?" To refuse to answer that question is to reject the Christ. What will YOU do with Jesus—right now, this very moment? *Today* is the day of salvation, NOW is the accepted time. "Boast not thyself of tomorrow; for thou knowest not what a day may bring forth" (Prov. 27:1).

Salvation is a gift, and the only way to come into possession of a gift is to receive it from the giver. God gave Jesus, who suffered, bled, and died, was buried, and rose again. He ascended, He now sits at the right hand of God the Father. Believe on Him, receive Him, He will save you —and you will know it!

"For by grace are ye saved through faith; and that not of yourselves: it is the gift of God: not of works, lest any man should boast" (Eph. 2:8,9).

". . . If thou shalt confess with thy mouth the Lord Jesus, and shalt believe in thine heart that God hath raised Him from the dead, thou shalt be saved. For with the heart man believeth unto righteousness; and with the mouth confession is made unto salvation. . . For whosoever shall call upon the name of the Lord shall be saved" (Rom. 10:9, 10,13).

"If we receive the witness of men, the witness of God is greater: for this is the witness of God which He hath testified of His Son. He that believeth on the Son of God hath the witness in himself: he that believeth not God hath made Him a liar; because he believeth not the record that God gave of His Son. And this is the record, that God hath given to us eternal life, and this life is in His Son. He that hath the Son hath life, and he that hath not the Son of God hath not life. These things have I written unto you that believe on the name of the Son of God; that ye may know that ye have eternal life, and that ye may believe on the name of the Son of God" (I John 5:9—13).

WHEN ALL LANGUAGE BREAKS DOWN

WHEN ALL LANGUAGE BREAKS DOWN

"And Saul, yet breathing out threatenings and slaugh-
er against the disciples of the Lord, went unto the high
riest, and desired of him letters to Damascus to the syna-
ogues, that if he found any of this way, whether they were
en or women, he might bring them bound unto Jerusalem.

"And as he journeyed, he came near Damascus: and
uddenly there shined round about him a light from heaven:
nd he fell to the earth, and heard a voice saying unto him,
aul, Saul, why persecutest thou me?

"And he said, Who art thou, Lord?   And the Lord said,
am Jesus whom thou persecutest: it is hard for thee to
ick against the pricks.

"And he trembling and astonished said, Lord, what wilt
hou have me to do?   And the Lord said unto him, Arise,
nd go into the city, and it shall be told thee what thou
ust do.   And the men which journeyed with him stood
peechless, hearing a voice, but seeing no man.   And Saul
rose from the earth; and when his eyes were opened, he
aw no man: but they led him by the hand, and brought him
nto Damascus. . . And Ananias. . .entered into the house;
nd putting his hands on him said, Brother Saul, the Lord,
ven Jesus, that appeared unto thee in the way as thou
amest, hath sent me, that thou mightest receive thy sight,
nd be filled with the Holy Ghost.

"And immediately there fell from (Paul's) eyes as it
ad been scales: and he received sight forthwith, and
rose,   and was baptized. . . *AND STRAIGHTWAY he
reached Christ in the synagogues, that He is the Son of
;od!*" (Acts 9:1–20 in part).

Thus the ninth chapter of Acts records the account of
he conversion of Saul of Tarsus, who became Paul, the
rince of Apostles.

In Acts 26:1–19 Paul makes his defence before King

Agrippa, and in giving his testimony he *recounts* his con version in minute detail. He knew exactly what he *saw*, what he *heard*, and what he *did*. He described his experi- ence on the Damascus road in glowing terms that left no part of it untold. Yet when the Holy Spirit called upon him to describe the Saviour, words failed him and he could only say, "Thanks be unto God for His UNSPEAKABLE gift!" (II Cor. 9:15).

I want us to consider three things which ALL LAN- GUAGE FAILS to describe:

Our Saviour,
Heaven's language,
Heaven's joy.

I.
Heaven's Unspeakable Gift—Our Saviour

Probably the outstanding thing in Paul's conversion experience was the light that shone round about him. He described it as brighter than the sun — (and Paul saw the light at midday when the sun was shining full strength). The light was so bright that it blinded him, and yet he found words to tell of it in his testimony.

But when he would tell us about the Saviour, the gift of God to hell-deserving sinners, words failed him and he could only say that the gift God gave to save sinners is *"unspeakable."* There are not enough words in all the languages of all the world to describe the Lord Jesus Christ.

There are three reasons *why* the Gift of God is "un- speakable":

A. *Because of who He was.* The Gift of God (Christ Je- sus) was God's Christ before He became man's Saviour. He was in the beginning with the Father (John 1:1,2), and according to John 1:3 and Hebrews 2:10 all things were made by Him. God created the worlds by Him. Jesus was very God (II Cor. 5:19). It is true that He was *man* just as surely and truly as WE are flesh; but He took upon Himself the *form* of man, and in that body of humiliation He became God's gift to this poor, lost world:

"For God so loved the world, that He gave His only begotten Son, that whosoever believeth in Him should not perish, but have everlasting life" (John 3:16).

In Genesis 3:15 God promised the seed of the woman to bruise the head of the serpent; and in Galatians 4:4,5 this promise was fulfilled: "But when the fulness of the time was come, God sent forth HIS SON, made of a woman, made under the law, to redeem them that were under the law, that we might receive the adoption of sons."

Jesus was very God, God's Christ—the seed of the woman in a body of humiliation, and in the fulness of time He came, the second Adam, to redeem all that the first Adam surrendered to Satan in the Garden of Eden.

Further proof of the identity of Jesus is found in the announcements God made concerning Him. God announced the birth of His Son in Luke 2:8–11:

"And there were in the same country shepherds abiding in the field, keeping watch over their flock by night. And, lo, the angel of the Lord came upon them, and the glory of the Lord shone round about them: and they were sore afraid. And the angel said unto them, Fear not: for, behold, I bring you good tidings of great joy, which shall be to all people. For unto you is born this day in the city of David a Saviour, *which is Christ the Lord.*"

God recognized and announced His Son at the beginning of His public ministry when Jesus was baptized of John in the river Jordan:

"And Jesus, when He was baptized, went up straightway out of the water: and, lo, the heavens were opened unto Him, and He saw the Spirit of God descending like a dove, and lighting upon Him: and lo a voice from heaven, saying, *This is my beloved Son, in whom I am well pleased*" (Matt. 3:16,17).

God recognized and announced His Son on the Mount of Transfiguration: "And after six days Jesus taketh Peter, James, and John his brother, and bringeth them up into an high mountain apart, and was transfigured before them: and His face did shine as the sun, and His raiment was white as the light. . . a bright cloud overshadowed them: and behold a voice out of the cloud which said, *This is my beloved Son, in whom I am well pleased; hear ye Him*" (Matt. 17:1—5 in part).

As Jesus drew near the end of His earthly ministry, He prayed, "Father, glorify thy name. Then came there a voice from heaven, saying, *I have both glorified it, and will glorify it again.* The people therefore, that stood by, and heard it, said that it thundered: others said, An angel spake to Him" (John 12:28,29).

At His birth, at His baptism, at the time of His transfiguration, and just before He went to the cross God publicly and audibly announced that Jesus was the Son of His love—yes, *very God*.

There is another announcement, found in Acts 2:32—36. In his sermon on the Day of Pentecost, Peter said, "This Jesus hath God raised up, whereof we all are witnesses. Therefore being by the right hand of God exalted, and having received of the Father the promise of the Holy Ghost, He hath shed forth this, which ye now see and hear. For David is not ascended into the heavens: but he saith himself, The Lord said unto my Lord, Sit thou on my right hand

30

until I make thy foes thy footstool. Therefore let all the house of Israel know assuredly, that *God hath made that same Jesus, whom ye have crucified, both Lord and Christ.*"

To those who read the Scriptures with an open mind, there is no doubt as to who Jesus was. He was man—yes, *truly man* except for man's sin; but He was also truly God, equal with God in every respect. In John 10:30 He announced, "*I and my Father are ONE.*"

B. Because of what He did. Christ the Son of God became Jesus, man's Saviour. In Matthew 16:26 He asked, "*What is a man profited if he shall gain the whole world— and lose his own soul? Or what shall a man give in exchange for his soul?*" Thus, the Saviour put the price of one sinner above the combined wealth of all the world — and yet, Jesus paid the sin-debt—not for just one sinner, but for "*whosoever will.*"

Volumes have been written about the Lord Jesus Christ —His ministry, His mission, His miracles. His *methods* have been discussed pro and con by the best of Bible scholars and by skeptics as well. But Luke describes His main mission in only one short verse: "*For the Son of man is come to seek and to save that which was lost*" (Luke 19:10).

It is true that Jesus was the greatest Teacher who ever lived. It is equally true that He was the greatest Healer of all time; He healed all manner of diseases, He even raised the dead. He was the greatest worker of miracles the world has ever known. But tremendous as are these facets of His ministry, they were only by-products coincidental with His primary mission on earth.

The Lord Jesus Christ left the bosom of the Father (John 1:18) and came into the world—not to *condemn* the world, but that the world through Him might be saved (John

31

3:16,17). He came into the world to give His life for the remission of sin (John 1:29; I John 2:2). His chief mission on earth was to settle the sin-question, pay the ransom, and set free those whom Satan held in the bondage of sin — and that is exactly what He did! He fulfilled every detail of His mission and completed the work God sent Him to do (John 19:30).

What did Jesus really DO with our sins? In I Peter 2:21,24 we read, ". . . Christ also suffered for us . . . Who His own self *bare our sins* in His own body on the tree, that we, being dead to sins, should live unto righteousness: by whose stripes ye were healed."

Notice the wording of this tremendous truth: *"He BARE our sins" — an act already accomplished.* In the tenth chapter of Hebrews we read that the law was but a shadow of things to come, and the offerings under the law could not *take away* sins: "For it is not possible that the blood of bulls and of goats should take away sins. . . But this man (Jesus), after He *had offered* one sacrifice for sins for ever, sat down on the right hand of God. . . For by one offering He *hath perfected* for ever them that are sanctified" (Heb. 10:4,12,14).

Christ will not bear our sins at some future date, nor is He in the process of bearing them now. He has *already borne* our sins. The sin-question is settled. The debt has been paid, redemption has been purchased, and now the question is, "What think ye of Christ? Whose Son is He?" The way you answer that question will determine whether you spend eternity in heaven or in hell:

"He that believeth on (Jesus) is not condemned: but he that believeth not IS CONDEMNED ALREADY, because he hath not believed in the name of the only begotten Son of God" (John 3:18).

32

Note further: By His stripes "ye WERE healed"—not "WILL BE healed," not "ARE BEING healed." I repeat: The sin-question is settled. The blood of Jesus Christ, God's Son, cleanses us from all sin. In His blood we have redemption, and the only thing any poor sinner can do to be saved is to receive the finished work of the Lord Jesus by faith. Without shedding of blood is no remission, but the shed blood of the Lamb of God saves and cleanses from all sin. If you are not saved, receive Him by faith, put your faith in His finished work, and the transaction is done!

C. *Because of the eternal results He accomplished.* "And without controversy great is the mystery of godliness: God was manifest in the flesh, justified in the Spirit, seen of angels, preached unto the Gentiles, believed on in the world, received up into glory" (I Tim. 3:16).

Jesus did what man could not do, He accomplished what the law could not accomplish: "For the law of the Spirit of life in Christ Jesus hath made me free from the law of sin and death. For what the law could not do, in that it was weak through the flesh, God sending His own Son in the likeness of sinful flesh, and for sin, condemned sin in the flesh: That the righteousness of the law might be fulfilled in us, who walk not after the flesh, but after the Spirit" (Rom. 8:2–4).

In Matthew 5:17,18 Jesus said, ". . . I am not come to destroy (the law), but to fulfil. For verily I say unto you, Till heaven and earth pass, one jot or one tittle shall in no wise pass from the law, till all be fulfilled." Since Jesus DID fulfill the law, He is therefore *"the END of the law"* to those who believe.

Repetition is in order here: Jesus settled the sin-debt —once, for all, eternally. He offered one sacrifice (Himself) for sins forever, never to be repeated. He poured out His own life, laid His life down for the sin of the world; and His sacrifice satisfied the heavenly Father so completely that today Jesus sits in the high seat of heaven (Heb. 1:3; 10:12—14). The results of what He did *eternally satisfied* the heart of God, the holiness of God, and the righteousness of God; and all who put their faith in the shed blood and the finished work of Jesus are justified freely from all things. They are just and holy in the eyes of a holy and righteous God. Study Romans 3:21—28.

"There is therefore now no condemnation to them which are in Christ Jesus, who walk not after the flesh, but after the Spirit" (Rom. 8:1).

"He came unto His own, and His own received Him not. But as many as received Him, to them gave He power to become the sons of God, even to them that believe on His name: Which were born, not of blood, nor of the will of the flesh, nor of the will of man, but of God" (John 1:11—13).

The results accomplished by the Lord Jesus Christ, God's gift to a lost world, are indescribable, unspeakable. There are not enough adjectives in all the languages of all the world to tell of the eternal results of what He did — and those results are ours *because of who He was and what He did.*

II.
Heaven's Unspeakable Language

Saul of Tarsus, converted in Damascus, became Paul the Apostle, minister to the Gentiles, and to him God revealed the mystery hidden through the ages but made known to the Church and the saints through God's revelation to Paul: "To whom God would make known what is the riches of the glory of this mystery among the Gentiles: which is Christ in you, the hope of glory" (Col. 1:27).

In II Corinthians 12:2—4 Paul said, "I knew a man in Christ above fourteen years ago, (whether in the body, I

34

cannot tell; or whether out of the body, I cannot tell: God knoweth;) such an one caught up to the third heaven. And I knew such a man, (whether in the body, or out of the body, I cannot tell: God knoweth;) How that he was caught up into Paradise, *and heard UNSPEAKABLE WORDS, which it is not lawful for a man to utter*!''

Most Bible scholars agree that the man of whom Paul speaks here was himself, and that the account refers to his ordeal at Lystra when he was stoned, dragged outside the city, and left for dead. It is believed that at this time Paul actually made the journey to Paradise and saw and heard what goes on there. He penned these words to the believers in Corinth, and from him we learn that the language of the third heaven, the Paradise of God, is unspeakable.

We learn that it was not lawful for man to speak on earth the words Paul heard in Paradise. If when he returned to earth he had announced what he had seen and heard, the saints would have become so homesick for heaven they would have been of no earthly good! They would have prayed for God to let them depart this mortal life immediately and be caught up into Paradise.

It is impossible to adequately describe heaven in terms which the finite mind of man can understand. John tells us of a city of pure gold, with twelve gates, each gate one giant pearl. If you will read the twenty-first chapter of Revelation you will see the foursquare city of God—such grandeur that the mind of mortal man cannot take it in in its fullest meaning. And since the language of heaven— language which *could* make known the wonders and glories of heaven—is unspeakable, the words in Revelation give us only a vague idea of the splendor and beauty of the place Jesus is now preparing for His own.

He said to His disciples, ''In my Father's house are many mansions . . . I go to prepare a place for YOU'' (John

14:2). The mansions in the Father's house were already there when Jesus made this announcement to His disciples. He has gone to prepare a place for US, and that place is the Pearly White City.

Paul found no way to speak the language of heaven— words that are unspeakable, unlawful for man to utter on this earth. I am so glad that one day I will hear heaven's language spoken by the Saviour who loved me so much that He willingly bore my sins in His own body on the cross that I might have life eternal!

III.
Heaven's Unspeakable Joy

"That the trial of your faith, being much more precious than of gold that perisheth, though it be tried with fire, might be found unto praise and honour and glory at the appearing of Jesus Christ: Whom having not seen, ye love; in whom, though now ye see Him not, yet believing, ye rejoice *with joy unspeakable* and full of glory" (I Pet. 1:7,8).

Believers are pilgrims and strangers on earth. We are IN the world, but not OF the world. We are journeying through this vale of darkness to a land that is fairer than day. We are often misunderstood, persecuted, and ignored— sometimes by even our own friends and loved ones. But in the midst of whatever grief, disappointment, and trials we meet on our earthly journey, we have joy that cannot be described in the language of man—*joy UNSPEAKABLE and full of glory!*

Just before His betrayal and arrest, Jesus said to His disciples, "These things have I spoken unto you, that *my joy* might remain in you, and that YOUR joy might be full!" (John 15:11). Every born again person possesses the Holy Spirit, the divine nature of God, and the joy of Jesus Christ (Rom. 8:9; II Pet. 1:4; John 15:11).

The joy in the bosom of a born again believer cannot be expressed in words. You need never attempt to tell a sinner how it feels to be saved, nor of the joy that floods the soul when Jesus comes into the heart. It is impossible for earth's language to express the joy the Christian possesses.

We possess divine nature. Positionally we sit together in heavenly places in Christ Jesus (Eph. 2:6,7). We are dead, and our lives are hid with Christ in God (Col. 3:3); and even though we are residing in a world that is not our home, we possess heaven's joy in our hearts — a joy UNSPEAKABLE!

If you do not have this joy, you can have it by simply believing in the finished work of Jesus, exercising faith in His shed blood, and asking Him to come into your heart. He will save you — and will give you joy, assurance, and peace such as the world knows nothing of, peace that surpasses all understanding.

If you ARE saved, but you are not enjoying your spiritual birthright, then yield your body a living sacrifice and your members as instruments of righteousness unto God. Allow Him to fill you with the Holy Spirit (Eph. 5:18), and you will know joy that is indescribable, *unspeakable* in words of man.

I will never cease to thank God for saving my soul, and for His goodness to me since I have been saved. I will never cease to thank Him for leading me and taking care of me throughout my earthly stay, and for the blessed assurance that I have a home in heaven. One day, when I see Him face to face, I will have a body just like HIS glorious body:

"Behold, what manner of love the Father hath bestowed upon us, that we should be called the sons of God:

37

therefore the world knoweth us not, because it knew Him not. Beloved, NOW are we the sons of God, and it doth not yet appear what we shall be: but we know that, when He shall appear, we shall be like Him; for we shall see Him as He is!" (I John 3:1,2).

If I had the opportunity of making *only one statement* on all the radio stations on earth, I think that statement would be: "*THANKS BE UNTO GOD FOR HIS UNSPEAKABLE GIFT!*"

THE FAITH THAT SAVES

THE FAITH THAT SAVES

"For by grace are ye saved THROUGH FAITH; and that not of yourselves: it is the gift of God: Not of works, lest any man should boast" (Eph. 2:8,9).

"... Faith toward our Lord Jesus Christ" (Acts 20:21).

We are saved by God's grace – God's unmerited, unearned, undeserved favor. Grace alone saves – but saving grace becomes ours only by faith–"faith toward our Lord Jesus Christ."

Saving faith always looks beyond the human and the present, to the divine and the eternal. Faith is never occupied with itself, but with *Him.* Faith's object is the Lord Jesus Christ, the only begotten Son of God, who willingly *laid down His life* that we might *have* life – and have it abundantly. Faith rests in Him (Jesus) AS Jesus, or as Saviour, the only begotten of the Father–He who is "full of grace and truth." Faith rests in Jesus and finds salvation from sin and eternal damnation, which are the just rewards of every sinner.

Faith receives Jesus as Christ–God's Christ, God's only begotten One. Faith accepts Jesus as the God-Man– flesh, yet divine; of the earth, yet from heaven; in a body, yet conceived of the Holy Ghost. Saving faith not only receives Jesus as Saviour, as Christ–God's begotten–but saving faith also receives Him as Lord. When one exercises saving faith, his experience does not stop with the new birth, but goes on to the fullness of the Spirit in submitting soul, spirit and body unto the Lord God Almighty.

Paul said, "I beseech you therefore, brethren, by the mercies of God, that ye present your bodies a living sacrifice, holy, acceptable unto God, which is your reasonable service" (Rom. 12:1). Salvation is a gift which becomes ours by faith in the virgin-born, divine Son of God, who died "according to the Scriptures," was buried "according to the Scriptures," and was raised "according to the Scriptures" (I Cor. 15:1–4). Saving faith allows the Lord to dominate the heart and daily conduct. Faith is like the ivy which clings to the giant oak in the forest. Faith lives because HE lives. Without faith it is impossible to please God (Heb. 11:6).

We might say that saving faith has feet, hands, eyes, and ears; and in this message I would like to discuss the feet, hands, eyes, and ears of saving faith:

I. FAITH IS THE FEET which come to Christ *simply because He calls.*

"Come unto me, all ye that labour and are heavy laden, and I will give you rest. Take my yoke upon you, and learn of me; for I am meek and lowly in heart: and ye shall find rest unto your souls. For my yoke is easy, and my burden is light" (Matt. 11:28–30).

Paul said, "Without faith it is impossible to please God," "By grace we are saved through faith," and "Faith cometh by hearing, and hearing by the Word of God." Jesus said, "Verily, verily, I say unto you, He that heareth my word, and believeth on Him that sent me, hath everlasting life, and shall not come into condemnation; but is passed from death unto life" (John 5:24).

Faith comes to Jesus simply because *Jesus said,* "Come unto me!" We do not ask WHY He loved us so—for there is no human answer. The love of God is far beyond our imagination; the finite mind of man cannot conceive of such a love. Even when we were yet sinners—wicked and ungodly—*God loved us.* God loved His enemies, the murderers of His Son, and He GAVE that Son to die for miserable, wretched, hell-deserving sinners. Such love cannot be understood by man, but faith can *appropriate* that love. Faith in the God of our Lord Jesus Christ brings salvation.

We love Him because He first loved us. Saving faith does not ask, "How is it possible?" or "Why should it be?" or "Is it real?" Saving faith comes to Jesus simply because Jesus said, "Come unto me!"

In Hebrews 6:18 Paul declares, ". . . It is impossible for God to lie . . . ." In Titus 1:2, we read, "In hope of eternal life, which *God, that cannot lie,* promised before the world began." If God is God, then He cannot lie. And if we believe that God IS, and that He is a rewarder of them who diligently seek Him, then we believe what God has said *simply because God SAID it!* And faith that saves has feet that come to Jesus simply *because He is Jesus* and because He said, "Him that cometh to me I will in no wise cast out" (John 6:37).

If you are not a believer, put the feet of faith in motion and come to Jesus, simply because He is Jesus and because He invites you to come. If you WILL come, He will under no circumstances cast you out. "Believe on the Lord Jesus Christ, and thou shalt be saved" (Acts 16:31).

2. FAITH IS THE HAND which *receives the gift of God.*

Our text again: "For by grace are ye saved, through faith; and that not of yourselves: *it is the gift of God....*" Jesus said, "For God so loved the world, that He gave His only begotten Son, that whosoever believeth in Him should not perish, but have everlasting life" (John 3:16).

Salvation is a gift. The fact that salvation is one hundred per cent God's gift to hell-deserving sinners is a truth clearly taught throughout the New Testament.

To make a gift possible, there must first be *a giver—*

one who is able to give and who has something TO give. There must also be a *gift*; the giver cannot give unless there is a gift to be given — and before that gift is complete, *there must be a receiver.* Regardless of how much I might have to give, if there is no one to receive it, it remains mine and therefore is not a gift. A gift is given by one who is able and willing to give, and who possesses something TO give; and then when one receives the gift from the giver, the transaction of giving is complete.

It was God the Father who so loved the world that He gave His only begotten Son, the Lord Jesus Christ, that whosoever (YOU and I) would receive Him and believe on Him should not perish, but have everlasting life. When the *feet of faith* bring us to Jesus, the *hand of faith* then reaches out to receive the gift of God—*simply because God gave*, willingly, unselfishly, *that we might be saved.*

The hand of faith asks no questions, seeks no explanations, demands no reasons. The hand of faith reaches out and receives the gift of God simply because God is love. God so loved the unrighteous and ungodly that He gave His only begotten Son—the most precious Jewel heaven held—that we poor, lost sinners might be saved from everlasting destruction.

I have been preaching the Gospel for 29 years — in churches, tents, tabernacles, and on the radio; and through these years the hardest thing for me to do is to get people to *believe and accept the truth that salvation is the gift of God*, and there is not one single thing the sinner can do to be saved except receive the finished work of the Lord Jesus. Just before He died, Jesus said, "It is finished!" (John 19:30). In Colossians 2:10 Paul tells us, ". . . Ye are complete in Him . . . ." If Jesus finished the plan of salvation and paid the sin-debt in full, and if we are complete in Him, then pray tell *what can be added to a finished work*? What can be added to completeness? "Christ in you, the hope of glory" (Col. 1:27). "If any man have not the Spirit of Christ, he is none of His" (Rom. 8:9). "Ye are dead, and your life is hid with Christ in God" (Col. 3:3).

If you are not born again, God grant that you receive Jesus this very moment, and He will "born" you into the family of God (John 1:11—13). Regardless of the value of a gift, regardless of what that gift may be, the only way a gift can become yours is for you to simply receive it from the giver, with thanksgiving. If you should give me a dollar—or ten dollars—as a gift, it would become mine only when *I received it* from you. Regardless of what a gift may be, the only way that gift can become yours is by your receiving it from the giver.

Dear sinner, you will surely burn in hell unless you receive the Lord Jesus Christ by faith. That is the only way to be saved. You cannot EARN your salvation; you cannot MERIT salvation; you cannot WORK FOR your salvation. Salvation is a gift — and the faith that saves exercises the hand of faith and receives the gift of God, simply because Jesus said, "God so loved the world, that He gave His only begotten Son, that whosoever believeth in Him should not perish, but have everlasting life."

3. FAITH IS THE EYE which *looks to Christ* and proves the truth of the words: "Look unto me, and be ye saved" (Isaiah 45:22).

It has been my privilege to travel on many foreign mission fields . . . Africa, Asia, South America, Mexico, and other places. Every religion on the face of this earth can be summed up under one of two headings: (1) Love, (2) Fear. Christianity is the true religion of love. All

45

others, regardless of how many there may be, can be put under the heading of *fear*. Christians serve God because they love Jesus. They look to Him for salvation, they look to Him for every need: *"Seek ye first the kingdom of God, and His righteousness; and all these things shall be added unto you"* (Matt. 6:33). *"My God shall supply all your need according to His riches in glory by Christ Jesus"* (Phil. 4:19). Christianity causes the believer to trust in the finished work of Jesus, relying entirely upon Him who is able to do exceeding and abundantly above everything that we think or ask, simply because He is God—all-powerful, all-seeing, ever-present.

Christianity removes the fear of the past, fear of the future, because we know that in Jesus our sins are covered by the blood and forgotten, never to be remembered against us any more. We know that we are more than conquerors through Him that loved us (Rom. 8:35–39). We know that He said, "I will never leave thee, nor forsake thee. So that we may boldly say, The Lord is my helper, and I will not fear . . ." (Heb. 13:5,6). We know that if we confess Him here on this earth, He will confess us before the Father: "Whosoever therefore shall confess me before men, him will I confess also before my Father which is in heaven. But whosoever shall deny me before men, him will I also deny before my Father which is in heaven" (Matt. 10:32,33).

The eye of faith is single—never double. We look to God through the Lord Jesus Christ (I Tim. 2:5; I John 2:1,2). Through Jesus, we look to God to save us, to sustain and keep us, to guide us, to supply our physical, financial and mental needs, our spiritual need – and our ETERNAL need! Jesus Christ is "the author and the finisher of our faith." We *believe that* because God said it (Heb. 12:2), and God cannot lie.

We do not look to feelings—but to fact: "Christ died for our sins—according to the Scriptures. He was buried and rose again the third day—according to the Scriptures" (I Cor. 15:1—4). We do not look to religion nor to the pope, the priest, the preacher, the evangelist, or the denomination. We look to the Lord Jesus Christ—the Christ of God, the only begotten of God: "For He hath made Him to be sin for us, who knew no sin; that we might be made the righteousness of God in Him" (II Cor. 5:21).

Yes, the eye of faith is single, looking to none other, depending upon none other, trusting in none other, save the Lord Jesus Christ—the all-sufficient, satisfying Saviour.

4. FAITH IS THE EAR which *hears His voice* and obeys His Word.

"Verily, verily, I say unto you, HE THAT HEARETH MY WORD, and believeth on Him that sent me, hath everlasting life . . ." (John 5:24). There is enough Gospel in that verse of Scripture to save the whole world if every sinner on earth would believe those words of Jesus.

John 5:24 is clear, to the point, and easily understood: *"He that heareth my word . . . ."* What does the Word tell us? The Word tells us that even when we were yet sinners, *Christ died for the ungodly.* The Word tells us that God so loved that He gave Jesus to die on the cross *"that whosoever believeth in Him"* should not perish in hell, but should have everlasting life. The Word tells us that *if we confess our sins, He is faithful and just to forgive us our sins* and cleanse us from all unrighteousness (I John 1:9). The Word tells us that *we are saved by God's unmerited, unearned, undeserved favor*—the gift of God, the grace of God, the Lord Jesus Christ. We are saved through His blood—not through our works: "Not by works of righteousness which we have done, but according to His mercy

47

He saved us, by the washing of regeneration, and renewing of the Holy Ghost" (Titus 3:5). The Word tells us that *we are complete in Him* (Col. 2:10). The Word tells us that *faith brings saving grace.* "Faith cometh by hearing, and hearing by the Word" (Rom. 10:17). Therefore, if we hear the Word of God and believe on the Lord Jesus Christ, we are saved!

Romans 10:13 is a marvelous verse: "FOR WHOSOEVER SHALL CALL UPON THE NAME OF THE LORD SHALL BE SAVED." Many times we ministers quote Scripture and forget to quote what precedes and what follows our text. Certainly it is a wonderful thing to read, "For whosoever shall call upon the name of the Lord shall be saved"; but we must not forget that Jesus said, "Not every one that saith unto me, Lord, Lord, shall enter into the kingdom of heaven; but he that doeth the will of my Father which is in heaven. Many will say to me in that day, Lord, Lord, have we not prophesied in thy name? and in thy name have cast out devils? and in thy name done many wonderful works? And then will I profess unto them, I never knew you: depart from me, ye that work iniquity" (Matt. 7:21—23).

Is there a contradiction of Scripture here? Paul said, "Whosoever shall call shall be saved"; but Jesus said, "Not everyone that saith, Lord, Lord — but he that doeth the will of my Father." No, there is no contradiction. We must read the remaining Scriptures that give us the full truth.

Paul said, "How then shall they call on Him in whom they have not believed? and how shall they believe in Him of whom they have not heard? and how shall they hear without a preacher? And how shall they preach, except they be sent? as it is written, How beautiful are the feet of them that preach the gospel of peace, and bring glad tidings of good things. . . So then *faith* cometh by hearing, and hearing by the Word of God" (Rom. 10:14,15,17).

There is our word "FAITH" again . . . the word that has feet, hands, eyes, and ears. Paul said, "Whosoever shall call upon the name of the Lord shall be saved"— and that is true; but *"how shall they call on Him in whom they have not believed?"*

Believing precedes calling — but notice: *"How then shall they believe in Him of whom they have not heard?"* So we see that hearing precedes believing, just as believing precedes calling.

But—*"How shall they hear without a preacher?"* God's preacher must preach before the sinner can hear. *"And how shall they preach, except they be sent?"* God sends ministers to preach the truth. The minister preaches the Word, the sinner HEARS the Word—and hearing the Word, faith is exercised in the heart. The sinner believes on Jesus, and then the lips *call unto salvation.*

In Romans 10:13–17 we see salvation in reverse: The preacher *preaches* the Word of God. The sinner *hears* the Word of God. *Faith* comes by hearing — and when faith is born in the heart, the unbeliever believes on the Lord Jesus Christ and thereby becomes a believer. Then automatically *he calls* — and "whosoever shall call upon the name of the Lord shall be saved"! Faith has an ear that listens only to Jesus. There are many, many gospels, but only one *saving* Gospel. There are many, many spirits—but only ONE true Spirit. That is why we are admonished to try the spirits to see if they be of God.

Summary: In this day of grace, God has called, anointed and ordained men to preach the Word. (Of course, Satan also has ministers, according to II Corinthians 11:13–15.) God's preachers preach the pure Gospel. With the *ear* of faith the sinner hears the Gospel and exercises the *feet* of faith, coming to the Lord Jesus for salvation. Coming to Jesus, the sinner reaches out the *hand* of faith and receives the gift of God, simply because God said, "Receive my Son – and thou shalt be saved."

The sinner, receiving the Lord Jesus, *looks to HIM* with the *eye* of faith for free, full, and complete salvation; having trusted Jesus, having become a son of God, he looks to Jesus for victory and for every need supplied. The true believer also looks *beyond this life* to that glorious day when Jesus will say to the Father, "This is my child; this is my son. He believed on me and trusted me. Therefore I confess him before thee, Father." Then the Father will say, "Enter thou into the joys of thy Lord"!

Dear reader, have you exercised faith in the finished work of the Lord Jesus? If you have not, God grant that this moment you bow your head, believe on the Lord Jesus Christ—"and thou shalt be saved." Receive Him as your Lord and Saviour, and you will be born into God's family. Come to Him, and He will in no wise cast you out. Put your faith in the finished work of Jesus this moment, and thank God for salvation!

"THE LORD IS MY SHEPHERD"

"THE LORD IS MY SHEPHERD"

The Twenty-third Psalm has probably been memorized by more Christians than has any other passage of Scripture in the Bible, with the exception of John 3:16. Yes, memorized — but not fully understood. Thousands know it by memory but not BY HEART. To "memorize" is to have it in one's memory; but to "know it by heart" is to know as personal Saviour and friend the Shepherd to which it refers.

There are one hundred and twenty words in the Psalm— six short verses, six sentences—and yet *volumes* could not contain its sweetness and truth. However, in a few short moments I want us to see if we cannot get just a little of the honey the Lord has in store (or should I say *stored up*) for us in this Twenty-third Psalm.

I want us to notice the first five words in the Psalm: "THE LORD IS MY SHEPHERD." On these words hinge all the rest of the Psalm; the other one hundred and fifteen words could not be spoken if the first five were not there. "The Lord is my Shepherd"—notice: "*MY Shepherd.*" The Psalmist believed in a personal Lord; David knew without a shadow of doubt that the Lord was *his*. He spoke those words out of a heart of assurance, and because of this assurance he could claim all of the rest of the Psalm. If you do not have the assurance of salvation, if you do not KNOW that the Lord is your Shepherd, then you cannot claim one promise of the Twenty-third Psalm.

"The Lord is my Shepherd; (*therefore*) *I shall not want.*" The comparison of God's care over His people to that of a shepherd with his flock is one that would naturally occur to David, who had himself been a shepherd.

The remembrance of the care of God over him recalled the extraordinary care which in earlier years he had extended to his flock (I Sam. 17:34,35). The idea which the language suggests is that of tender care, protection and provision for their wants. The words "SHALL NOT WANT," as applied to the Psalmist, would embrace everything that could be a proper object of desire—whether temporal or spiritual; whether pertaining to the body or the soul; whether having reference to time or to eternity. There is no need to suppose that David limited this to his temporal necessities, but the idea manifestly is that God would supply ALL needs, ALWAYS. There is something wrong when a man is always down and out. I know there are times when the way grows mighty dark; but regardless of how dark the way or how hard the times, if the Lord is our Shepherd we will always emerge more than conquerors over the wolves and lions of hell that would devour us.

Verse two begins by saying, "He (MY Shepherd) *maketh me to lie down in green pastures.*" The literal Hebrew says, "Pastures of tender grass." That is, the Good Shepherd provides only that which is best for His sheep. The picture of flocks lying down in green, tender grass is one of calmness and repose. "He maketh me to lie down" signifies *rest*; but that is not the only idea presented here: The flocks lie down *amidst abundance . . . fully fed and satisfied.*

Verse 2 continues, *"He leadeth me beside the still waters."* "*Still* waters"—not stagnant, not tempestuous and stormy—but calm and restful. How wonderful it is, in the hustle and bustle of this old fast-living world, to be led beside still waters, to know One who can give calmness of soul in the midst of this world's turmoil! That One is Jesus Christ, "the great Shepherd of the sheep, through the blood of the everlasting covenant" (Heb. 13:20).

Is your life one of sin and strife? Are the winds of the world and the billows of sin beating against your soul? Then I beg you to let the Good Shepherd lead you out of troubled waters into the still waters of God's great love.

Verse 3: *"He restoreth my soul . . . ."* Literally, *"He causes my life to return."* If I fail, stumble, or wander away, the Good Shepherd seeks me and brings me back. If I lose my joy and peace through negligence and sin, the God I love seeks me out and draws me back (through many avenues which it would take another sermon to discuss). As the Shepherd of my soul He is anxious over me and wants to restore my soul. He has promised that "If we confess our sins, He is faithful and just to forgive our sins and to cleanse from all unrighteousness." This applies not only to wandering or backsliding from God, but also to the Christian whose life or spirit is exhausted, weary, troubled, anxious, worn down with care and toil. Are you thus wearied, cast down and discouraged? Then look to Jesus, who will restore your soul. He will encourage you and fill you with new joy, new life, and inspire you with a new effort to travel on. If you can say with assurance, "THE LORD IS MY SHEPHERD," you can claim this promise, knowing that He *will* restore your soul.

When He has restored my soul, He does something else for me: *"He leadeth me in the paths of righteousness for His name's sake"*—for His own sake, that His name might be honored. As a Christian, I bear His name. (The name *Christian* is simply a nickname given to the followers of Christ when they went to Antioch—Acts 11:25. They were called Christians because they lived and acted so much like the Christ; the word *Christian* means *Christ-like.*) I bear the name Greene because I was born into the Greene family; I am a Christian because I am God's child by birth

55

. . . the *new* birth. My earthly father did not want me to disgrace his name — and neither does my heavenly Father want me to disgrace *His* name. Therefore, "He leadeth me in paths of righteousness"—not that I might brag and boast, but *for His name's sake*, that He might be honored. Romans 8:9—14 says, "If any man have not the Spirit of Christ, he is none of His. . . For as many as are led by the Spirit of God, they are the sons of God." God's Holy Spirit leads me into the right paths. The feeling expressed by the Psalmist is that of confidence in God and assurance that He will always lead His people in the path in which they should go. This He will always do if men will follow the directions of His Word and the leading of His Spirit. None that thus submit to Him ever go astray.

Verse 4: *"Yea, though I walk through the valley of the shadow of death, I will fear no evil . . . ."* What a comforting statement! What a comforting truth made possible by the Shepherd of our soul. David knew that "it is appointed unto men once to die," and he could declare that he had no fear of death because His Lord would go with him all the way. You see, "THE LORD IS MY SHEPHERD" took all the fear out of death for David. Notice carefully the wording of the verse: Did David say, "Yea, though I walk through the VALLEY OF DEATH"?? No, he said, ". . . the VALLEY OF THE SHADOW of death," and that makes quite a difference. *Shadows* do not hurt us, but the real object *kills*. Sinners die! Yes, they die eternally — but Christians only pass through the SHADOW.

In I Corinthians 15:55 Paul says, "O death, where is thy sting? O grave, where is thy victory?" He then answers, "The sting of death is sin; and the strength of sin is the law." In the heart of a Christian, the sin question has been settled. Sin has been removed — therefore, the sting of death has been taken out. The Good Shepherd, the Lord Jesus Christ, satisfied the heart of God concerning the law; He fulfilled every jot and every tittle of the law; He fulfilled every demand of a holy God: therefore, for those who trust Him, He has removed the sting of death. Child of God, knowing this should relieve you of all fear and dread of death. For further assurance the Psalmist says, *"For thou art with me."* You will not be alone; God will be your protector, your companion, your guide through the Valley of the Shadow of Death. What a promise! What a Saviour who is *able* to fulfill that promise!

"Thy rod and thy staff they comfort me." With this staff the Shepherd rules and guides the sheep to green pastures and defends them from evil. With it He also feels out the way in dangerous places. I am so glad we have the rod of the Lord Jesus and the staff of the Holy Spirit to lean upon. The blessed Holy Spirit has already felt out the way for the children of God, and He will lead us in that path each step of the way.

Verse 5 begins with *"Thou preparest a table before me in the presence of mine enemies"*! Thank God for the prepared table that our wonderful salvation provides—yes, even in the presence of our enemies. When our enemies would down us and damn us, the Good Shepherd feeds us in their very presence — and they cannot prevent it. They are compelled to look on and see how God intercedes in behalf of His own, and how He provides for and defends them. *"If God be for us, who can be against us?"*

"Thou anointest my head with oil; my cup runneth over." Not only does God provide our temporal needs, but He provides for the soul as well. In the Scriptures oil refers to the Holy Spirit. Therefore, if our head is anointed with oil we should have the fruit of the Holy Spirit in our life. What is the fruit of the Spirit? The Bible answers

very definitely: "But the fruit of the Spirit is Love - Joy - Peace - Longsuffering - Gentleness - Goodness - Faith - Meekness - Temperance."

So, the Good Shepherd anoints our heads with love. "God is love," and when we know Him in the forgiveness of sin He plants within our hearts love for everybody. It is impossible for the Lord Jesus and hatred to dwell in the same heart. John says, "We know that we have passed from death unto life because we love the brethren." Love is one of the outstanding fruits of the Holy Spirit. Then, the Good Shepherd anoints us with joy. Peter refers to it as "Joy unspeakable and full of glory." John says it is our spiritual birthright to have "full joy"; and thank God, the anointing of peace comes with knowing the Lord as our Shepherd. No wonder the Psalmist says, "My cup runneth over"! Whose cup would *not* run over, knowing that he possessed all this in knowing the Lord as his personal Saviour?

The last (but by no means least) verse in this great psalm: *"Surely goodness and mercy shall follow me all the days of my life: and I will dwell in the house of the Lord for ever."* Who could ask for more? As we said in the beginning, the truth of the first verse makes all this possible. If the Lord is our Shepherd, then we *know* goodness and mercy shall follow us all the days of our life.

Goodness: The Word of God says, "No good thing will He withhold from them who walk uprightly." Good things are promised to those who serve the Lord. Again: "Every good gift and every perfect gift is from above, and cometh down from the Father of lights." Every good thing that comes our way is from the Lord. The devil has nothing to offer but heartaches, heartbreaks, sadness, sorrow— and at last eternal hell-fire for those who serve him. *The*

Lord is the Giver of good gifts.

Mercy: "And mercy shall follow me all the days of my life." I am glad God does not deal with His sheep according to their just reward. He deals in mercy—*unusual* mercy! (Psalm 108:4; Eph. 2:4). I am glad also that this mercy is for *"all the days of my life."* God does not have mercy for a season and then change His mind; but He, "Having loved His own, *loved them to the end*"!

"And I will dwell in the house of the Lord for ever." Yes, because the Lord is my Shepherd, I shall dwell in the house of the Lord forever. What a promise! What an inheritance! What a glorious occasion to look forward to! No wonder Peter said that knowing Him whom we have not seen brings "joy unspeakable and full of glory." There are not enough words in the English language to describe the joy and glory that await the child of God. Paul says, "Eye hath not seen, nor ear heard, neither have entered into the heart of man, the things which God hath prepared for them that love Him." Heaven—the eternal sheepfold of God's sheep—cannot be described in words. Paul said he was "caught up to the third heaven and heard things and saw things that are not lawful to tell." No one but a loving, forgiving Shepherd could give a hell-deserving sinner the right to dwell in the house of the Lord forever . . . "forever" . . . think of it!

Can you say: "The Lord is MY Shepherd"? If you can, then you can claim every promise of this great psalm. If He is *not* your Shepherd, then you cannot claim any one of His precious promises.

If you do not know the Lord Jesus as your Shepherd, I pray that you will bow your head right now and trust Him as your Lord. All you need to do to get into the sheepfold of God is confess your sin and ask Jesus to save you.

59

THE THREEFOLD BLESSING OF SALVATION

THE THREEFOLD BLESSING
OF SALVATION

"Giving thanks unto the Father, which hath made us meet to be partakers of the inheritance of the saints in light; Who hath delivered us from the power of darkness, and hath translated us into the kingdom of His dear Son: in whom we have redemption through His blood, even the forgiveness of sins" (Col. 1:12—14).

These verses contain the threefold blessing of salvation by grace through faith in the finished work of Jesus; but they belong only to born again, blood-washed believers. They do not belong to anyone who is not washed in the blood and saved by grace. They are part of the title deed to our inheritance, and they belong ONLY to the children of God.

If you are not a believer, if you are living in sin, God grant that this message will create within your soul a thirst for the water of life—a desire to know Jesus, whom to know aright is life eternal.

The children of God are a blessed people, a peculiar people, a heavenly people. We are pilgrims and strangers in this land; we are looking for a city whose Builder and Ruler is God, and at the end of life's journey we will hear Him say, "Enter thou into the joys of thy Lord."

Let me point out the threefold blessing of our salvation:

I.

In verse 14 of our text we read, *"In whom we have redemption through His blood, even the forgiveness of sins."* What a clear statement! What a gold mine of blessing! And what makes it so wonderful is the fact that this wealth of blessing becomes ours *because of a Person*.

It is not through a system, a ritual, or a man-made program that we have forgiveness of sins, but *through and IN* a Person—the Person of God's only begotten Son, who left the bosom of the Father, took a body of flesh, and in that flesh became the mighty Victor of Calvary.

It was *God's Son* who laid His life down to save sinners. It was not an angel—nor any other of the heavenly beings—who brought redemption down to man. It was the Son of God's love who left the glory He had with the Father; left the beauties of heaven and the singing of the angels, to take upon Himself a body of flesh and become obedient unto death, even the death of the cross. Jesus stepped from heaven's glory to the most shameful death one could die, to secure for us at the infinite cost of His blood this boundless wealth of divine blessing; and this blessing is *for all who will believe on His name* and put their faith and trust in His shed blood.

There is only *one Person* who can meet the need of the sinner and bring the love of God into the sinner's heart, and that one Person is Jesus, "in whom we have redemption through His blood, *even the FORGIVENESS OF SINS*.' It is clearly taught in the Scriptures that "ALL have sinned, and come short of the glory of God" (Rom. 3:23) and that "there is none righteous, no, not one" (Rom. 3:10)

If you are not born again, saved by the grace of God then you are a sinner. You cannot *deny* that you have sinned, for Almighty God has placed within you a conscience to remind you that you DO sin. If you are not a child of God, then even as you read these lines your conscience reminds you of some dark sin, perhaps *many* sins in your past.

For many unsaved people, there are "skeletons" in the closet of the soul, hidden from the eyes of man but naked before the eyes of God. Dear sinner friend, if dark sins haunt you, if many times they have brought tears to your eyes and fear that has caused you to tremble, there IS hope, there IS a way of escape for you — but ONLY ONE WAY! Thank God, that Way is open and free, and ALL sinners are invited to enter and claim sins forgiven in the blood of Jesus.

Your sins may be many, they may seem black and terrible in your own eyes; but God has provided *forgiveness for all* in the blood of Jesus. Oh, yes, there are many religions — *but remember:* The devil is the archenemy of every individual on the face of this earth; it is his desire to damn as many souls as possible, and he enjoys telling the sinner that all anyone need do to be saved is to join some church, live a good life, and be baptized.

Satan is the father of lies! God has made it clear in His Word that "there is none other name under heaven given among men, whereby we must be saved" (Acts 4:12). Jesus said to Thomas, *"I am the Way, the Truth, and the Life: No man cometh unto the Father, but by ME"* (John 14:6).

There is salvation in no other. Jesus is the ONLY WAY. He is the only one who can forgive sins, and He is the only one who satisfied God the Father, thus making it possible for God to be just and yet justify the ungodly through the blood of Jesus Christ, the sinless Son.

When a sinner puts his trust in the blood of Jesus Christ, he puts himself *under the shelter* of the blood. God saves sinners for Christ's sake (Eph. 4:32); and he who puts his faith in the finished work of Jesus, stands before God the Father, *sheltered by the blood* that satisfied God's holiness and God's righteousness.

Our redemption is in a PERSON. Paul said, ". . . I know WHOM I have believed" (II Tim. 1:12). Paul believed in WHOM — not *what.* Many church members know WHAT they believe, but they do not know HIM in WHOM we have redemption.

There are believers who worry and fret about their sins. If they would only *believe the Word of God* they would be delivered from worry and anxiety, because we have redemption on the ground of the finished work of Jesus, and through His shed blood our sins are removed from us as far as the east is from the west (Psalm 103:12).

Our standing before God is not measured by church membership, water baptism, good works, or anything else that man can be, give, or do. Our standing with God is determined by a Person – the Lord Jesus Christ – whose blood was shed for the remission of sins and whose blood covers us when we believe in Him as Saviour.

As believers, we need to see our *present position* in Christ: We are sons of God—NOW (I John 3:2). We possess divine nature—NOW (II Pet. 1:4). We possess the Holy Spirit—NOW (Rom. 8:9,14,16; Eph. 4:30).

And where is our SAVIOUR now? The *tomb* could not hold Him. He arose, He ascended, He lives to die no more (Rev. 1:18). "Who . . . when He had by Himself purged our sins, *sat down on the right hand of the Majesty on high*" (Heb. 1:3). Our redemption is in HIM — therefore: As believers, we are dead, and our lives are hid with Christ in God—NOW (Col. 3:3). We sit together in heavenly places in Christ Jesus—NOW (Eph. 2:6). Our citizenship is in heaven, we are in Christ, Christ is in us; and we are "accepted in the Beloved" on the grounds of His shed blood and finished work.

"Not by works of righteousness which we have done, but according to His mercy He saved us, by the washing of regeneration, and renewing of the Holy Ghost" (Tit. 3:5).

Jesus paid our sin-debt in full through the sacrifice He offered once, for all, forever, never to be repeated.

Therefore, the blood of Jesus Christ, God's Son, cleanses us from ALL sin; and in Jesus we stand before God justified, cleansed, sanctified, holy — fit for the kingdom of heaven.

Redemption is ours *now*, our redemption is in Christ, and Christ is seated at the right hand of God the Father. Therefore we are positionally just as sure for heaven as if we were already there, because *in Jesus we ARE already here.* We are His purchased possession through the price of redemption. We are adopted into the family of God as heirs of God and joint-heirs with Christ. God has accepted us because sin's debt was paid on Calvary through the shed blood of His Son, Jesus Christ.

Redemption is not something we are hoping for or looking forward to — we are redeemed NOW; we are NOW sons of God. We are looking forward to that glorious morning when we will see Jesus and be like Him. That is the hope of the believer.

II.

In verse 13 of our text we read, *"WHO hath delivered us from the power of darkness and hath translated us into he kingdom of His dear Son."* Again, the personal pronoun "WHO" refers to a Person, not a program, not a religion.

All unbelievers dwell in the kingdom of darkness, which is the kingdom of Satan. Jesus said, "I am the light of the world" (John 8:12). Satan is the exact opposite of Jesus; he is the author of darkness. All unbelievers are children of Satan; they live in the kingdom of darkness.

Writing to the believers in Ephesus, Paul said, "And you hath He quickened, who were dead in trespasses and sins: wherein in time past ye walked according to the course of this world" (the course of this world is darkness), "according to the prince of the power of the air, the spirit that now worketh in the children of disobedience:

Among whom also we all had our conversation in times pas
in the lusts of our flesh, fulfilling the desires of the flesh
and of the mind; and were by nature the children of wrath'
(children of darkness), "even as others. BUT GOD, who
is rich in mercy, for His great love wherewith He loved us
even when we were dead in sins, hath quickened us" (made
us alive) "together with Christ, (by grace ye are saved;
and hath raised us up together, and made us sit together in
heavenly places in Christ Jesus" (Eph. 2:1—6).

Unbelievers are dead in trespasses and sins — and
there is no light in the dead; they are in total darkness
Unbelievers walk after the things of darkness. Men love
darkness rather than light because their deeds are evil
They follow after the prince of the power of the air, the
prince of darkness. They walk in the spirit of disobedience
the spirit of darkness. The conversation of the unbeliever
is in lust; the desires of the unbeliever are born of darkness—desires of the flesh. The very nature of the sinner
is the nature of darkness because the sinner is a child of
the devil (John 8:44).

But God, who so loved the world that He gave His only
begotten Son, through His great love and His rich mercy
has raised us from the dead and made us alive. He has
taken us out of the kingdom of darkness and placed us over
into the kingdom of light. When unbelievers put their trust
in Jesus, God takes them out of the family of Satan and
places them over into the family of God. They are trans
lated from the family of darkness into the family of light

"But of HIM are ye in Christ Jesus, who of God is
made unto us wisdom, and righteousness, and sanctification, and redemption; that, according as it is written, He
that glorieth, *let Him glory in the Lord*" (I Cor. 1:30,31).

Here is exactly what happens when a person is saved
Jesus said, "Verily, verily, I say unto you, He that heareth

my word, and believeth on Him that sent me, hath everlasting life, and shall not come into condemnation; but is passed from death unto life" (John 5:24).

When the sinner hears the Word, believes and receives the Word, the *power* of the Word "borns" the unbeliever into the family of God; and that very moment God literally takes the unbeliever out of darkness and places him into the kingdom of light: ". . . As many as received Him, to them gave He power to become the sons of God, even to them that believe on His name: Which were born, not of blood, nor of the will of the flesh, nor of the will of man, but of God" (John 1:12,13).

"Being born again, not of corruptible seed, but of incorruptible, by the Word of God, which liveth and abideth for ever" (I Pet. 1:23).

"Of His own will begat He us with the Word of truth, that we should be a kind of firstfruits of His creatures" (James 1:18).

"But ye, brethren, *are not in darkness*, that that day should overtake you as a thief. *Ye are all the children of light, and the children of the day: We are not of the night, nor of darkness.* Therefore let us not sleep, as do others; but let us watch and be sober. For they that sleep sleep in the night; and they that be drunken are drunken in the night. But let us, *who are of the day*, be sober, putting on the breastplate of faith and love; and for an helmet, the hope of salvation." (Our hope is in the return of Jesus.) "For God hath not appointed us to wrath, but to obtain salvation by our Lord Jesus Christ" (I Thess. 5:4—9).

Please notice the language of the Holy Spirit here: Believers are NOT in darkness. Believers are the children of LIGHT—NOW. We are not looking forward to the day when we WILL BE in the light, it is not something we are reaching out after or striving toward. We possess the light

NOW, we have *already been delivered* from the power of darkness.

We are not saved through our goodness, through religion or church membership, nor through practicing rituals or following the traditions of men; but when we hear the Gospel, believe on the Lord Jesus Christ and put our trust in His shed blood for the remission of sins, *that moment* He redeems us, delivers and sanctifies us. We are hidden in Christ in God and sealed by the Holy Spirit until the glorious day of redemption when we will see Jesus face to face. We are looking for that blessed hope and the glorious appearing of our great God and our Saviour, Jesus Christ, who gave Himself for us that He might redeem us and purify unto Himself a peculiar people, zealous of good works.

III.

In verse 12 of our text, we read, "*. . . Giving thanks unto the Father, which hath made us meet to be partakers of the inheritance of the saints in light.*"

It is right to praise Jesus for saving us. It is right to give testimony to the salvation we possess, the joy we have, and the needs that are met for us in Jesus. But beloved, we should not forget that it was GOD THE FATHER who loved us in the beginning, even before the foundation of the world. God the Father so loved sinners that He planned and perfected salvation through the blood of the Lamb without spot or blemish.

In I Peter 1:18—25 we have a clear picture of redemption. Peter tells us that we were not redeemed with corruptible things, but with the precious blood of Christ, "*who verily was foreordained before the foundation of the world,*" but was manifest in these last times for us.

"But we see Jesus, who was made a little lower than the angels for the suffering of death, crowned with glory and honour; that He by the grace of God should taste death

70

for every man" (Heb. 2:9). We are justified by faith, we have peace with God through the Lord Jesus Christ, and it is by Him that we have access by faith into grace. We rejoice in hope of the glory of God—"And not only so, but we also JOY IN GOD through our Lord Jesus Christ, by whom we have now received the atonement" (Rom. 5:11).

God the Father, through His grace, allowed Jesus the Son to come into the world and take a body of flesh, and in that body do what the law could NOT do because of the weakness of the flesh. What the first Adam lost through the weakness of the flesh, the last Adam (the Lord Jesus Christ) bought back at the tremendous price of His blood. But it was God the Father who turned His head while His Son paid the sin-debt.

Jesus willingly bore our sins in His own body on the cross (I Pet. 2:24; John 10:18). God has pardoned us; we are exonerated (acquitted) in the blood of Jesus through His finished work. God reckons us righteous when we believe on the Lord Jesus Christ and put our faith in His finished work.

"But to him that worketh not, but believeth on Him that justifieth the ungodly, his faith is counted for righteousness. Even as David also describeth the blessedness of the man, unto whom God imputeth righteousness without works" (Rom. 4:5,6).

By God's grace, through the great love wherewith He loved us and through the finished work of Jesus the Son, God the Father has made us meet to enter glory. Nothing less could satisfy the heart of God. What God demanded, God provided in Jesus; and since we have redemption in His blood, since we have been translated from darkness into light and from the family of Satan into the family of God, we are meet to enter the Father's house and dwell in the Pearly White City — and God's purpose in it all is

71

*"That in the ages to come, He might shew the exceeding
riches of His grace in His kindness toward us through
Christ Jesus"* (Eph. 2:7).

It is in God's eternal plan to have many sons around
Himself in His house, and through the shed blood of Jesus
THE Son, *He will have many sons.* Throughout eternity
the "many sons" made white in the blood of the Lamb will
live in the light of God's own holiness and love. We who
believe on THE Son shall dwell in the company of *many
sons* in that glorious land that is fairer than day; but even
while we travel this pilgrim journey on earth, we have the
Spirit of sonship, crying, "Abba, Father."

All born again believers NOW possess a threefold
blessing:

1. Whose sins are forgiven, who are redeemed from all
    the power of Satan.
2. Who are delivered from the world, the flesh, and dark-
    ness.
3. Who are made meet for the celestial city, the Father's
    house.

BELIEVERS AND UNBELIEVERS—THEIR FUTURE

BELIEVERS AND UNBELIEVERS –
THEIR FUTURE

"He that believeth and is baptized shall be saved; *but he that believeth not shall be damned*" (Mark 16:16).

"He that believeth on Him is not condemned: *but he that believeth not is condemned already, because he hath not believed in the name of the only begotten Son of God*" (John 3:18).

Regardless of what men preach, teach, or write, there are only two classes of men: Believers and unbelievers . . . saved and lost. There is no middle ground with God. We are either a son of God (I John 3:1–3), or we are a child of the devil (John 8:44). There is no mistake concerning Bible language here.

". . . God is light, and in Him is no darkness at all" (I John 1:5). Please notice—*God is light*. In God there is *no darkness at all*. There is no gray, no twilight, no partial light. God is blazing brilliance, Shekinah glory— whiteness indescribable in the language of man. Therefore, "if we walk in the light, as He is in the light, we have fellowship one with another, and the blood of Jesus Christ His Son cleanseth us from all sin" (I John 1:7).

The Bible points out an undeniable difference between believers and unbelievers. The future for believers and for those who are NOT believers is vastly different, and that difference can be clearly seen in the Word of God if we study with an open heart and an open mind. The sad thing today is that many church people study the Bible to prove religious points instead of studying to enlighten their hearts. There is no passage in the Word of God that points out the difference between believers and unbelievers any clearer than Hebrews 9:27: ". . . It is appointed unto men once to die, but after this the judgment." Peter tells us, "The Lord knoweth how . . . to reserve the unjust unto the day of judgment to be punished" (II Pet. 2:9). Therefore, according to the Word of God, the outlook for unbelievers is dark and dismal. Clouds of impending judgment hang heavily over their heads, and *"the wrath of God abideth on them"* (John 3:36). The outlook of the unbeliever is nothing but darkness, despair, and destruction: *"He that believeth not is condemned already . . ."* (John 3:18).

But to the believer, God gives this blessed assurance: "So Christ was once offered to bear the sins of many; and unto them that look for Him shall He appear the second time without sin unto salvation" (Heb. 9:28).

Just as truly as it is appointed unto men once to die, and after death the judgment, it is true that Christ was offered to bear the sins of many, and to those *who look for Him* He shall appear the second time without sin, unto salvation. ". . . God hath not appointed us to wrath, but to obtain salvation by our Lord Jesus Christ" (I Thess. 5:9). We are assured that we have an inheritance "incorruptible, undefiled, that fadeth not away," but this inheritance is reserved in heaven for us "WHO ARE KEPT BY THE POWER OF GOD THROUGH FAITH UNTO SALVATION READY TO BE REVEALED IN THE LAST TIME" (I Pet. 1:3–5).

The unbeliever has nothing to look forward to but his appearing before Christ to be judged and condemned; the unbeliever is reserved unto judgment. But the believer is looking for that blessed hope and the glorious appearing of the great God, and when He appears we shall be like Him (Titus 2:13; I John 3:1–3). We shall then receive our inheritance that cannot corrupt, is not defiled, which cannot pass away, and is reserved in heaven for us who are kept by God's power.

The sinner is appointed unto wrath; the believer is appointed to an inheritance *reserved.* Anyone who is willing to study these tremendous truths with an open mind and an open heart will readily see that there is as much difference between these two appearings and these two reservings as there is between Christ and the devil, salvation and wrath, joy and misery, heaven and hell, light and darkness, holiness and sin. There is no middle ground. It is either the light of Shekinah glory or the darkness of hell; the life of Christ or the death of sin. There is an undeniable difference between believers and unbelievers, so far as their future outlook is concerned. Are you a believer?

The believer is assured of the correcting hand of God: "But when we are judged, we are chastened of the Lord, that we should not be condemned with the world. Wherefore, my brethren, when ye come together to eat, tarry one for another. And if any man hunger, let him eat at home; that ye come not together unto condemnation. And the rest will I set in' order when I come" (I Cor. 11:32–34). If you will study this entire chapter in I Corinthians you will learn that the reason God chastens the believer is that he should not be condemned with unbelievers: ". . . *We are chastened of the Lord, that we should not be condemned with the world."*

The Lord refuses to allow His people to run wild; He stops them in one way or another: "For whom the Lord loveth He chasteneth, and scourgeth every son whom He receiveth. If ye endure chastening, God dealeth with you as with sons; for what son is he whom the father chasteneth not? But if ye be without chastisement, whereof all are partakers, then are ye bastards, and not sons'' (Heb. 12:6–8).

In I Corinthians 11:32 the Scripture suggests two alternatives:

1. Condemnation with the world.
2. NOT being condemned with the world.

The latter applies to believers. In this tremendous truth we see that when the world is condemned, when "the world passeth away, and the lusts thereof," *the children of God will be where condemnation cannot reach them.* In Isaiah's day, God cried out, "Come, my people, enter thou into thy chambers, and shut thy doors about thee: hide thyself as it were for a little moment, until the indignation be overpast" (Isaiah 26:20).

Note three things in this verse:

1. God's people are invited to enter into their innermost chamber.
2. They are commanded to shut the doors about them.
3. Thereby they hide themselves.

Likewise, *believers are dead*, and their lives are "hid with Christ in God" (Col. 3:3). We are covered by the blood of the Lamb, and that blood cleanses from all sin. We are hidden in the atonement; we are shut in, in the perfection of His finished work, by the blood of His cross and the power of His resurrection. We are kept by the power of God; the wrath and indignation of His holiness will pass over us because we are covered with and protected by the blood. "When I see the blood, I will pass over you" (Exodus 12:13).

Positionally, the believer sits together with Christ in heavenly places (Eph. 2:6). We are "hid with Christ in God" (Col. 3:3). We are "kept by the power of God" (I Pet. 1:5). Because of the blood of His cross, there is therefore now no condemnation, nor can condemnation ever be heaped upon the believer hidden in Christ in God.

"Who shall lay anything to the charge of God's elect? It is God that justifieth. Who is he that condemneth? It is Christ that died, yea rather, that is risen again, who is even at the right hand of God, who also maketh intercession for us" (Rom. 8:33,34). Condemnation can never reach Jesus. Therefore, condemnation can never reach the believer who is in Christ, the hope of glory (Col. 1:27).

The believer is in Christ as Noah and his family were in the ark. The ark protected them from the avenging flood sent by God, displaying His wrath and destruction against sin. *Christ is the Ark* that protects US from the wrath of God and His righteous indignation against sin. In Christ we are safe; out of Christ there IS no safety! Jesus bore our sins in His own body on the cross (I Pet. 2:24). Therefore, He took our place; He satisfied the holiness of God — and in Him we are just as safe as Noah and his family were safe in the ark as it rode the flood waters and preserved them in the hour of destruction.

In Jesus, believers are as safe as were the children of Israel in their homes behind the door sprinkled with blood. Jesus is the Lamb whose blood was shed for the remission of sin—which blood, being sprinkled on the doorpost and lintel of our heart and conscience, speaks peace to us. ("Being justified by faith, we have peace with God"—Rom. 5:1.) When we are covered by the blood, *we are just as safe as the blood that covers us*, because God the Father, in His holiness, sees the *blood*.

In Jesus the believer is safe, just as Rahab was safe in her house with the scarlet thread displayed. The scarlet thread of Rahab assured protection from the judgment God was about to pour out upon Jericho; and that scarlet thread pointed to the precious blood of the Lord Jesus

Christ, which gives assurance to the believer. Jesus died willingly for the sin of the world, and the question of our sin will never be brought up again. God has forgiven and forgotten our sins. He has put them behind His back, covered them as with a thick, dark cloud, and cast them into the depths of the sea, *to remember them against us no more.* The record is eternally forgotten and will never be brought out against any believer. But when the UNBELIEVER stands before God, the books will be opened and sinners will be judged out of the things written in the books (Rev. 20:12).

The believer—in Christ, covered by the blood, hid in God, seated in heavenly places—*cannot be reached.* Sin with its condemning power cannot reach those who are under the blood. Jesus settled the sin-debt; and the Law with its terrible curse cannot condemn the believer, because "Christ is the end of the law for righteousness to every one that believeth" (Rom. 10:4). Justice with its righteous and holy demands cannot reach the believer, because Jesus (who knew no sin) was made sin for us, that we in Him might be made the righteousness of God (II Cor. 5:21). Satan with his lying, accusing voice cannot reach the believer, because Jesus destroyed him who had the power of death (Heb. 2:9,14). The believer cannot be reached by all the forces of hell with its burning flame, its biting, stinging, never-ending death, because *Jesus conquered death, hell, and the grave,* and has in His possession the keys of hell and of death (Rev. 1:18). The world, with all of its deceptive lust and alluring temptations, cannot reach the believer, who is hid with Christ in God. We are more than conquerors through Him that loved us! (Rom. 8:35—39).

The believer has unshakable assurance; but the unbeliever lives in fear. "He that believeth on Him is not condemned . . ." (John 3:18). "We know that we have

80

passed from death unto life, because we love the brethren" (I John 3:14). "If any man have not the Spirit of Christ, he is none of His. . . As many as are led by the Spirit of God, they are the sons of God. . . His Spirit beareth witness with our spirit, that we are the children of God" (Rom. 8:9,14,16).

". . . IS NOT CONDEMNED!" These are positive words. The original language reads, "Is not judged." The believer is not sentenced to condemnation or death; therefore he can never be condemned. It is true that all have sinned and come short of the glory of God; it is true that the wages of sin is death, and the soul that sinneth shall surely die. Sin is the only thing that *could* condemn us, but Jesus willingly bore our sins in His own body on His cross (I Pet. 2:24). Therefore, when we are in Christ Jesus, the sin-question is settled forever. Jesus paid the sin-debt, and in Him we are free from the condemnation of sin. We have this assurance, because "He that believeth on Him *is not condemned.*"

Every true believer is predestined "to be conformed to the image of His Son, that He might be the firstborn among many brethren" (Rom. 8:29). Here is unshakable assurance for the believer: ". . . *God hath not given us the spirit of fear; but of power, and of love, and of a sound mind.* . . For I know whom I have believed, and am persuaded that He is able to keep that which I have committed unto Him against that day" (II Tim. 1:7,12).

Clearer words than these have never been spoken. God does not give the spirit of fear to any child of His. He gives the spirit of power, the spirit of love, the spirit of a clear, sound, understanding mind, knowing WHOM (not *what*) we have believed. Many people know WHAT they believe, but they do not know WHOM (Jesus). He is a *person*, not a system. There are many religious systems, but these do not bring assurance or hope; only Christ can do that. Therefore, if we know WHOM (Jesus), we know that *He is able*. Knowing that He is able, we readily admit that *we are UNABLE*.

In the language of Paul we say, "I know that in me (that is, in my flesh,) dwelleth no good thing" (Rom. 7:18). We also say with Paul, "Let him that thinketh he standeth take heed lest he fall" (I Cor. 10:12). But when we know WHOM (Jesus), we know that HE (Jesus) is able, because He was tempted in all points as we are, yet was without sin. He overcame the world, the flesh, and the devil; death, hell, and the grave. He ever lives to mediate (I Tim. 2:5; I John 2:1,2). Therefore, when we know HIM, we have unshakable assurance. But Paul goes a step further:

"He is able to keep THAT which we have committed unto Him." Just what does "THAT" consist of? Anything and all things which we commit to Him—soul, spirit, body, time, talent, health, or wealth. Jesus is able to keep WHATEVER we place in His hands by faith. How much have we committed unto Him? The extent to which we commit will determine the abundance of our Christian joy. Jesus came that we might have life—*abundant* life (John 10:10).

How long will He keep THAT? *How long* is He able to keep whatever we place in His hands? He is able to keep it "against that day"—the day when we stand before Him to receive rewards for stewardship — *not* whether we are saved or lost, but the *sort of works* that we have done (I Cor. 3:11–15). The believer who knows WHOM he has believed (Jesus), and confesses that He is able to keep (and WILL keep) all that is committed to Him against that day, has unshakable assurance.

If you do not know that you are saved as truly and assuredly as you know you are breathing, I would certainly hate to die with your species of religion. If you are saved, you are alive unto God, hid with Christ in God. You possess the Holy Spirit; you are led by the Holy Spirit, assured by the Holy Spirit, sealed by the Spirit, and you sit together in heavenly places in Christ Jesus. Therefore it is utterly impossible for any person to be saved and not know it. If you do not know you are saved, bow your head this moment, "believe on the Lord Jesus Christ, and thou shalt be saved."

What does it mean to believe on the Lord Jesus Christ? It simply means to believe from the heart that He paid sin's debt and purchased redemption through His blood. He beckons, "Come unto me, and I will in no wise cast you out" (John 6:37). And if you will by faith simply place your life in the hands of Jesus, believing that He is able to save, keep, and present you to the Father in that day, He will save you. Place yourself in His hands as you place yourself in a chair when you sit down to rest. Put in Jesus the faith that you put in the chair when you trust the weight of your body to it. If you will put that same faith in the finished work of Jesus, He will save you now!

The divine promise to believers is unmistakable. The outlook of the unbeliever is clear.

To the believer, the promise is, "Verily, verily, I say unto you, He that heareth my word, and believeth on Him that sent me, hath everlasting life, and shall not come into condemnation; but is passed from death unto life" (John 5:24).

Please note: *"HATH everlasting life"* — not "WILL HAVE," but "ALREADY HATH." There is no supposition about this unmistakable promise: *"Shall not come into condemnation."* The believer is saved and sure for heaven. Salvation is determined by faith in God. Rewards are earned by faithful stewardship.

"We are more than conquerors through Him that loved us" (Rom. 8:37).

"Sin shall not have dominion over you" (Rom. 6:14).

"There hath no temptation taken you but such as is common to man: but God is faithful, who will not suffer you to be tempted above that ye are able; but will with the temptation also make a way to escape, that ye may be able to bear it" (I Cor. 10:13).

Read carefully Romans 8:31--39. In these verses we are clearly taught that there is no power in heaven, on earth, nor under the earth that can separate us from the love of God which is in Christ Jesus. It is appointed unto men once to die, and after death—*the judgment.* It is the common lot of all men to die; but Christ was once offered to bear the sins of many, and unto them that look for Him He shall appear the second time without sin unto salvation. Death and judgment are the common lot of humanity. All have sinned and come short of the glory of God (Rom. 3:23). There is none righteous, no, not one. All we like sheep have gone astray. But Jehovah laid on Jesus the iniquity of us all (Isa. 53:6). Christ died the death; He paid the ransom note and purchased our redemption. He is the atonement for our sins—and not for ours only, but for the sins of the whole wide world. All who will believe shall be saved; but all who refuse to believe shall be damned!

"The wicked shall be turned into hell, and all the nations that forget God" (Ps. 9:17). "The wages of sin is death" (Rom. 6:23). "When lust hath conceived, it

84

bringeth forth sin: and sin, when it is finished, bringeth forth death" (James 1:14,15). The promise is clear, sure, and unmistakable: *"Believers shall not come into condemnation."* Believers have everlasting life; they are protected by the blood, led by the Spirit, kept by the power of God, and will be confessed by our Confessor, the Lord Jesus Christ, who ever liveth to make intercession for us (Matt. 10:32; I Tim. 2:5; I John 2:1,2).

The gift of God is unspeakable (II Cor. 9:15); therefore, it provides an unspeakable privilege.

"Whosoever shall confess that Jesus is the Son of God, God dwelleth in him, and he in God. And we have known and believed the love that God hath to us. God is love; and he that dwelleth in love dwelleth in God, and God in him. HEREIN IS OUR LOVE MADE PERFECT, that we may have boldness in the day of judgment: because as He is, so are we in this world. There is no fear in love; but perfect love casteth out fear: because fear hath torment. He that feareth is not made perfect in love. We love Him, because He first loved us" (I John 4:15–19).

To the believer, the day of judgment does not hold fear and dread; but the UNBELIEVER has nothing to look forward to but certain judgment and condemnation. The unbeliever lives in the fear of that day when he will stand before a holy God. There is no peace, no perfect confidence, and no unshakable hope *except through faith in the Lord Jesus Christ.*

The ground of our confidence and assurance concerning the day when we stand before God is because even as He (Jesus) is, we also are in this world; and He will not in that day condemn those who are like Himself. Believers are righteous as HE is righteous. The believer is in Christ (Eph. 1:1; Col. 2:10); not only in Christ, but hid with Christ in God (Col. 3:3), and sealed by the Holy Ghost until the day of redemption! (Eph. 4:30). The believer is led by the Holy Spirit into paths of righteousness (Rom. 8:14; Psalm 23). Christ is made unto us wisdom, righteousness, sanctification, and redemption (I Cor. 1:30). Christ is our righteousness; we are one with Him, and positionally we sit with Him now in heavenly places (Eph. 2:6). All that belongs to Jesus belongs to us—not because of our righteousness, but *because of the love of God* and His unspeakable gift to us, the Lord Jesus Christ.

"Perfect love casteth out fear." Believers are perfected in the love of God so that we may have confidence and assurance without fear in the day of judgment. *The unbeliever lives continuously in fear*, knowing that he has an appointment with a holy God and that he will receive a just reward—*the reward of eternal death*. Revelation 21:8 lists the occupants of hell, and the first name on the list is ". . . *the fearful.*" All unbelievers *live* in fear, *die* in fear, and spend eternity in the madhouse of fear, among leaping flames and screaming spirits.

Who is he that condemneth? "What shall we then say to these things? If God be for us, who can be against us? He that spared not His own Son, but delivered Him up for us all, how shall He not with Him also freely give us all things? Who shall lay anything to the charge of God's elect? It is God that justifieth. Who is he that condemneth? It is Christ that died, yea rather, that is risen again, who is even at the right hand of God, who also maketh intercession for us" (Rom. 8:31–34).

Who CAN condemn the believer? Can *God the Father* condemn us? No, God the Father has justified us for Jesus' sake (Eph. 4:32). Can *Christ* condemn us? No. It was Christ who died for us. He loved us when we were yet without strength, when we were ungodly sinners and enemies to God. Therefore, He who died for us will not condemn us if we put our trust in His shed blood. Can *the Holy Spirit* condemn us? No. He called us, He draws us, He "borns" us into the family of God (John 3:5). The Holy Spirit indwells us, leads us, seals us, and He will quicken us in the first resurrection. The Holy Ghost who is one with the Father and the Son in our salvation will not, *cannot*, condemn us.

Can *the devil* condemn us? No, because *Jesus conquered the devil.* Satan cannot condemn the believer because Jesus broke his power and conquered him who had the power of death. "Forasmuch then as the children are partakers of flesh and blood, He also Himself likewise took part of the same; that through death He might destroy him that had the power of death, that is, the devil; and deliver them who through fear of death were all their lifetime subject to bondage" (Heb. 2:14,15).

Can *the Law* condemn us? No. "For Christ is the end of the law for righteousness to every one that believeth" (Rom. 10:4).

Can *death* condemn us? No. Christ conquered death and has the keys (Rev. 1:18). He removed the sting of death (I Cor. 15:54—57). To the brokenhearted sisters at the tomb of Lazarus Jesus said, "He that believeth in me, though he were dead, yet shall he live: and whosoever liveth and believeth in me shall never die" (John 11:25,26). The sting of death, the fear of death, the power of death, the destruction of death have been taken care of by our Saviour in whom we believe.

In Romans 8:35 Paul asked, "Who shall separate us from the love of Christ?" And then he names many powers and possibilities. But in verses 38 and 39 of that chapter he cries out, "I AM PERSUADED, that neither death, nor life, nor angels, nor principalities, nor powers, nor things present, nor things to come, nor height, nor depth, NOR ANY OTHER CREATURE, shall be able to separate us from the love of God, which is in Christ Jesus our Lord!"

There is no condemnation to the believer, because Christ died—yea, rose again, and even this moment sits at the right hand of God the Father to make intercession for believers. "Believe on the Lord Jesus Christ, and thou shalt be saved" (Acts 16:31). Believe on the Lord Jesus Christ—and thou shalt overcome the world, the flesh and the devil (I John 5:4,5). Believe on the Lord Jesus Christ, confess Him before men, and He will confess you before the Father which is in heaven (Matt. 10:32,33).

It is the spiritual birthright of every believer to enjoy the fullness of God's grace—abundant living and unshakable assurance. He that believeth — is *saved*. He that *believeth not* shall be damned.

Are you a believer? Have you put your faith in the finished work of Jesus? If not, you are already condemned. The wrath of God hangs over your head. The cancer of sin is slowly eating away the very opportunity you now have to be saved. Unbeliever, bow your head, and in your own words tell Jesus you do believe He died to save sinners; invite Him into your heart, and He will save you NOW! There is therefore *now* no condemnation to them which are in Christ Jesus — but condemnation is *already* the portion of the unbeliever. The only thing between you and the leaping flames of a devil's hell is the few short days you have to live.

ASSURANCE

ASSURANCE

"And this is the record, that God hath given to us
ternal life, and this life is in His Son. He that hath the
on hath life; and he that hath not the Son of God hath not
fe. These things have I written unto you that believe on
e name of the Son of God; that ye may know that ye have
ternal life, and that ye may believe on the name of the Son
f God" (1 John 5:11–13).

The subject of this message is one of vital importance.
should be proclaimed from every pulpit today. *Assurance*
as much to do with the joy and peace of the Christian —
et there are many professing Christians who do not seem
 have a definite understanding *concerning* assurance.
hey live on supposition and "hope-so." No person will
ver enjoy his (or her) spiritual birthright until he has
blessed assurance" in his heart.

The New Testament doctrine of the believer's perfect
ssurance has been sadly neglected. After twenty-eight
ears in the ministry (twenty-five of those years preaching
aily on the radio), I have learned much through dealing
ith different people concerning a "know-so" experience
f Grace.

When asked, "Are you saved? Are you born again?"
 great percentage of church members will reply, "I guess
o . . . I hope so . . . I think I am," or "I expect to be
aved in the end." Such answers reveal the distressing
act of gross Bible ignorance among church people, and
ring an alarming realization of the misunderstanding of
iod's Holy Word concerning assurance. Every born again
hild of God should know beyond the shadow of a doubt
at he has experienced a miracle in his heart. The Bible

91

calls that miracle *the new birth* (*salvation*). If a person
does not definitely know that he has experienced salvation, the Bible fact is clear that, while he may have joined
a church or united with some religion, he certainly is not
saved.

IS IT POSSIBLE FOR A TRUE BELIEVER TO DOUBT?

I believe it is possible for a truly born again child of
God to doubt or question his salvation, but that time of
doubt will come AFTER his experience with God and it
will be of short duration.   There must be a time when the
Christian KNOWS he is saved, a time when he has a definite experience and positive assurance of salvation. Later
it is possible for Satan to plant doubt in the mind of that
born again one.   But the Holy Spirit who dwells within will
shortly reassure, and remove the doubt.   If you have not
had a definite time in your life when you KNEW you were
saved, then you are not saved.   The primary desire of the
devil is to damn souls; but if a sinner believes on the Lord
Jesus Christ and is saved, Satan does not give up . . . he
simply attacks from another angle and does everything in
his devilish power to rob the believer of his spiritual birthright.

Jesus not only came that we might have life, but that
we might have life *abundantly*; and if the devil can cause
us to doubt, he can keep us from enjoying our spiritual
birthright. *It is a sin to doubt*; it is a sad state for a saved
person to be in — and *it is the work of the devil*! Satan is
a liar from the beginning. He is a powerful personality and
seems to have a great deal of influence over some believers, in that he causes them to put question marks around
the simple Word of God. However, when a truly born again
believer doubts, it is never for very long; and even in the
moment of doubt, there is assurance deep down in the heart
of that believer.   The Spirit bears witness when we are

born of the Spirit.

Very few of us give the devil credit for the power and wisdom he has. He knows a doubting child of God will never become an effective soul winner — and certainly we are saved to tell others! God saves us to serve the Lord Jesus, to point sinners to the Lamb of God. A doubting Christian cannot and will not become a soul winner.

In the first chapter of Job we have the account of a day when the sons of God "came to present themselves before the Lord, and Satan came also among them." The Lord asked Satan, "Whence comest thou?" Satan replied in these words, "From going to and fro in the earth, and from walking up and down in it."

The Lord then asked Satan if he had considered Job— "a perfect and an upright man," one who feared God and hated evil. The devil accused the Lord of *paying* Job to serve Him: "Hast not thou made an hedge about him, and about his house, and about all that he hath on every side? Thou hast blessed the work of his hands, and his substance is increased in the land. But put forth thine hand now, and touch all that he hath, and *he will curse thee* to thy face!"

You know the story. God permitted the devil to take everything Job had—*except his life.* In the face of the severe calamity that befell him, Job did *not* curse God. Instead, he said, *"Though He slay me,* yet will I serve Him!"

In Revelation 12:7—10 we read: "And there was war in heaven: Michael and his angels fought against the dragon; and the dragon fought and his angels, and prevailed not; neither was their place found any more in heaven. And the great dragon was cast out, that old serpent, called the Devil, and Satan, which deceiveth the whole world: he was cast out into the earth, and his angels were cast out with him. And I heard a loud voice saying in heaven, Now is come salvation, and strength, and the kingdom of our

93

God, and the power of His Christ: for the accuser of our brethren is cast down, which accused them before our God day and night."

Satan is the accuser of the brethren. He slanders the sons of God to the heavenly Father, and in turn slanders God to the Christian. Satan tells God that His sons are crooked and no good — and then turns right around and tells God's children that God is a liar and will not keep His promise. That is the major ministry of Satan in this present hour. The sinner is lost, doomed, with only one heartbeat between himself and hell. Satan knows that, and tries to keep Christians in a turmoil of doubt so that they will be so occupied with doubt they will not try to win souls to Christ. They will be unfruitful.

The only way a believer can bear much fruit and thereby glorify God (John 15:1–8) is to abide in the Father and the Son. You may rest assured that an *abiding* believer will not doubt. If we abide we have confidence, assurance, and perfect peace because our mind is resting in Jesus (Isaiah 26:3).

The doubter does not doubt *himself* . . . he does not doubt his sincerity nor his honesty: *He doubts God.* God clearly states in His Word that if we confess our sins, He will *forgive* our sins. If we call upon His name He will save us, and "whosoever" comes to the Father will not be cast out. Yet, we confess our sins, we call on God, we come to Him and ask Him to save us—*and then doubt that He does what He declares He will do!* By so doing, we do what Satan did in the Garden of Eden — we call God a liar.

In Genesis 2:17 God said to man, ". . . for in the day that thou eatest thereof THOU SHALT SURELY DIE."

In Genesis 3:4, Satan replied to this declaration: "And the serpent said unto the woman, Ye shall *not* surely die!"

God said, "You eat — you die!"

94

Satan said, "You eat — you will *not* die!"

That is Satan's polite way of saying, "Your God is a liar. You are not going to die. Go ahead, eat the fruit— *and be wise!*" Eve believed the devil, she ate, she gave to Adam and he ate — and through the disobedience of one man death moved upon *all* men. But thank God — through the obedience of the second Adam (the Lord Jesus) life is possible for "whosoever will."

If you have bowed your head and in your heart asked God to have mercy on you, forgive your sins and save you— and yet you doubt that you have ever been saved, you are calling God a liar. Perhaps you think that statement is too harsh — but suppose we hear the Word of God:

"He that believeth on the Son of God hath the witness in himself: he that believeth not God HATH MADE HIM A LIAR: because he believeth not the record that God gave of His Son" (I John 5:10).

Face it: ". . . God so loved the world, that He gave His only begotten Son, that whosoever believeth in Him should not perish, but have everlasting life" (John 3:16). To *hear* that truth and yet *reject* it, is to refuse to believe the record of God. To refuse to believe the record of God concerning His only begotten Son is to make Him a liar.

During the transition period, many were confused concerning what they should or should not eat, as having to do with the Law of Moses. Referring to the eating of doubtful meats, Paul tells us, ". . . HE THAT DOUBTETH IS DAMNED if he eat, because he eateth not of faith: for *whatsoever is not of faith is sin!*" (Rom. 14:23).

The wages of sin is death. No sin shall enter heaven. So if we doubt that God provided redemption in Jesus; if we doubt that faith in Jesus is enough to save us; if we doubt the Word of God—the plan of salvation as laid down

in the Word of God—then we will be damned. We cannot be
saved any way except the Bible way of God's grace,
through faith in the finished work of Jesus — His death,
burial, and resurrection (I Cor. 15:1-4).

Many professing Christians doubt and lack assurance
because they depend upon their *feelings* instead of trusting in the Word of God. They had rather put their salvation on the grounds of emotional experiences than to rest
on the Chief Cornerstone (the Lord Jesus) and the sure
foundation of the Word of God. Is it "feelings"--or the
blood of Jesus Christ--that saves from sin? Will "feelings" take you to heaven, dear friend? Feelings vary; but
the Word of God never changes . . . Jesus Christ never
changes . . . the blood never changes. From everlasting
to everlasting, God is God — He changes not. He is the
same yesterday, today, and forever (Psalm 90:1,2; Heb.
13:8).

"Feelings" can change with the weather; feelings
change with age. Then why should anyone be so foolish
as to *rely upon feelings* to get into the Pearly White City?
It is true some people become very happy—filled with joy—
when they accept Christ, while others do not reveal their
emotions through the avenues of laughter, tears, waving
their arms—and a hundred other emotional demonstrations.
Yet the person who weeps or laughs is no more saved than
those who do *not* weep or laugh, if both place their faith
in the finished work of the Lord Jesus Christ. *Feelings*
have to do with the nervous system—the body, the flesh,
the mind. *Salvation* goes deeper than that: Salvation is
in the heart:

"Christ in you, the hope of glory" (Col. 1:27).

"There is therefore now no condemnation to them
which are in Christ Jesus" (Rom. 8:1).

"We are dead, and our lives are hid with Christ in

God" (Col. 3:3).

"Whereby are given unto us exceeding great and precious promises: that by these ye might be partakers of the divine nature . . ." (II Pet. 1:4).

"If any man have not the spirit of Christ he is none of His" (Rom. 8:9).

"Except a man be born of the Spirit, he cannot enter into the kingdom of God" (John 3:3,5).

"The flesh profiteth nothing." Man looks on the outward appearance; he measures religious experiences and religious depth by emotional demonstrations and good works; but God looks on the heart.

There is no Scripture that guarantees salvation on the grounds of *feelings* — but there are many Scriptures that guarantee eternal life on the basis of faith—faith in God, faith in the finished work of Jesus, faith in the Word. "Verily, verily, I say unto you, He that heareth my word, and believeth on Him that sent me, hath everlasting life, and shall not come into condemnation; but is passed from death unto life" (John 5:24).

If you have been looking for feelings, trusting in feelings; if some days you feel saved, and other days you do not feel saved, may God help you to stop trusting in feelings and stand on John 5:24. Personally, I stand on Romans 10:9. More than twenty-eight years ago I put my trust in Christ on the authority of that verse: "That if thou shalt confess with thy mouth the Lord Jesus, and shalt believe in thine heart that God hath raised Him from the dead, thou shalt be saved." I did that — and I am standing on it . . . resting in the truth of it. I know I will be in the heavenly family when we sit down at the marriage supper in the sky!

If you have sincerely confessed your sin to God; if you have earnestly called on God to save you, then you should be ashamed to doubt God! To be sure, when you were a sinner you *had* no doubts . . . you had nothing TO DOUBT! You had never made a profession of faith, you had never united with the visible church, you had not followed Christ in baptism, you had never testified, you had never said to anyone, "I am saved, I am a Christian." You were dead in trespasses and sins. You *had* no "feelings." But when Jesus came in and saved you, the devil declared war — and the spirit of Satan has been fighting and warring against the Spirit of the living God who abides in your bosom. You should be ashamed of yourself, to let the devil whisper in your ear that God did not keep His Word. God promised — and if you called in sincerity, God saved you . . . and you should *not doubt it*!

EVERY BELIEVER CAN ENJOY
PERFECT ASSURANCE

Perfect assurance can be yours through the Word of God:

"These things have I written unto you that believe on the name of the Son of God; *that ye may know that ye have eternal life*, and that ye may believe on the name of the Son of God" (I John 5:13).

The assurance that we possess eternal life is most assuredly and completely set forth in God's written Word. *Feelings* have nothing to do with assurance. The written Word of God who cannot lie brings assurance. Nothing changes more rapidly nor more often than do our feelings; but the Word of God "is forever settled in heaven." A true believer does not "hope" or "think" that he has eternal life. A true believer KNOWS it! You not only *have* eternal life—but you KNOW you have eternal life, just as surely as you know you have physical life. To doubt God's Word is to doubt God, because "In the beginning was the Word, and the Word was with God, and the Word was God . . . and the

Word became flesh . . ." (John 1:1,14).

I say frankly that if you cannot trust God's Word, you cannot be saved, because it is only through the Word that we *can* be saved:

"And I give unto them eternal life; and they shall never perish, neither shall any man pluck them out of my hand" (John 10:28).

"The thief cometh not, but for to steal, and to kill, and to destroy: I am come that they might have life, and that they might have it more abundantly" (John 10:10).

". . . The gift of God is eternal life through Jesus Christ our Lord" (Rom. 6:23).

"In Him was life; and the life was the light of men" (John 1:4).

"He that believeth on the Son hath everlasting life: and he that believeth not the Son shall not see life; but the wrath of God abideth on him" (John 3:36).

"Verily, verily, I say unto you, He that believeth on me hath everlasting life" (John 6:47).

"He that hath the Son hath life . . ." (I John 5:12).

"But to him that worketh not, but believeth on Him that justifieth the ungodly, his faith is counted for righteousness" (Rom. 4:5).

"Not by works of righteousness which we have done, but according to His mercy He saved us, by the washing of regeneration, and the renewing of the Holy Ghost" (Titus 3:5).

The Word of God brings saving faith. The Word of God is the seed that brings forth eternal life (Rom. 10:17; I Peter 1:23).

EVERY BELIEVER HAS ASSURANCE THROUGH THE HOLY SPIRIT

Jesus said, "No man can come to me except the

Father which hath sent me draw him" (John 6:44). The Father draws the sinner through (or by) the Holy Spirit: "Nevertheless I tell you the truth; It is expedient for you that I go away: for if I go not away, the Comforter will not come unto you; but if I depart, I will send Him unto you. And when He is come, He will reprove the world of sin, and of righteousness, and of judgment: of sin, because they believe not on me; of righteousness, because I go to my Father, and ye see me no more; of judgment, because the prince of this world is judged" (John 16:7–11).

God the Father draws the sinner to the Son. The drawing power is the Holy Spirit. When the sinner is convicted and drawn by the Holy Spirit, He (the Holy Spirit) works the miracle of the new birth: "Except a man be born of . . . the Spirit, he cannot enter into the kingdom of God" (John 3:5).

"If any man have not the Spirit of Christ, he is none of His" (Rom. 8:9). It is utterly impossible to become a child of God apart from the birth and possession of the Holy Spirit. The Holy Ghost convicts us, draws us, "borns" us, indwells us—and gives to us blessed assurance.

". . . As many as are led by the Spirit of God, they are the sons of God. For ye have not received the spirit of bondage again to fear; but ye have received the Spirit of adoption, whereby we cry, Abba, Father. THE SPIRIT HIMSELF beareth witness with our spirit, that we are the children of God" (Rom. 8:14–16).

I say without reservation, if you cannot bow your head and ask the heavenly Father, "Am I saved? Am I truly born again?" and receive an affirmative answer in the inner man, through the Holy Spirit's witnessing with your spirit that you are a child of God, it is a sure sign you have never been born again. God is no respecter of persons, and if He gives the witness of the Spirit to one of

lis sons, He will give the witness to each and every one
vho is born of the Spirit.

Do you have the witness of the Spirit? If you do not,
iod grant that you bow your head this moment and ask
lim to save you and put within you the blessed Holy Spirit.

The work of the Holy Spirit does not stop there. He
onvicts us, He draws us, He borns us, He indwells us,
le assures us, and then, thank God, He fills us (Eph. 5:18)
nd seals us until the day of redemption (Eph. 4:30).

EVERY BELIEVER HAS ASSURANCE
THROUGH THE NEW MAN PUT WITHIN HIS BOSOM
AT THE NEW BIRTH

". . . If any man be in Christ, he is a new creature:
ld things are passed away; behold, all things are become
ew" (II Cor. 5:17).

When a person is born again, God, through the opera-
on of the Holy Spirit, removes the old sinful heart and
uts in a brand new heart: "A new heart also will I give
ou, and a new spirit will I put within you. I will take
way the stony heart out of your flesh, and I will give you
 new heart" (Ezek. 36:26).

From the heart proceed the issues of life. When we
re saved, God puts within us a new life, a new creation.
le puts a new heart—a new man—in our bosom.

Hear these solemn words: "My little children (Chris-
ians, believers, sons of God), let us not love in word,
either in tongue; but in deed and in truth. And hereby
ve know that we are of the truth, and shall *assure our*
earts before Him. For if our heart condemn us, God is
reater than our heart, and knoweth all things. BELOVED,
F OUR HEART CONDEMN US NOT, THEN HAVE WE
ONFIDENCE TOWARD GOD" (I John 3:18–21).

Here the Word clearly teaches that the heart of a

101

believer assures the believer that all is well with Go
and if your heart condemns you, you are not saved. Fa
it — and do something about it!

In closing let me say it is the spiritual birthright
every believer to enjoy abundant life; and it is a trick
the devil to *rob* believers of their spiritual birthright.
you do not have perfect assurance in your heart concer
ing your salvation, get on your knees—and *stay there* unt
you can say, "My heart condemns me not. The Spirit wi
nesses with my spirit that I am a child of God because
believe the Word of God!"

NEVER FORGET: "These things have I written un
you that believe on the name of the Son of God; that y
may know that ye have eternal life, and that ye may b
lieve on the name of the Son of God" (I John 5:13).

OUR WORRIES — CHRIST'S PEACE

OUR WORRIES – CHRIST'S PEACE

"Peace I leave with you, My peace I give unto you . . ." (John 14:27). This was Christ's last will and testament. This was His only legacy – He had nothing else to bequeath to His children. He had become the poorest of the poor, the most humble of the humble. He had no material possessions of any kind to divide among His disciples. The men who followed Him loved Him, and He loved them so tenderly! So He bequeathed to them something this world can never give, something money cannot buy: HE GAVE HIS PEACE. He who was rich became poor, that we through His poverty might become rich—with riches the world cannot understand or know—the riches of His peace.

Peace is a priceless possession. Multimillionaires cannot buy it, learning and wisdom will not acquire it. Jesus bequeathed to His followers a possession that only He can give. *Only Jesus* can give peace – and please bear in mind it IS a GIFT . . . it cannot be earned, merited, nor purchased.

In the day and hour in which we live, it is certainly not easy to achieve inner peace. In this world, I think there are special demons to torment the minds of the children of God. If it were possible, Satan would disturb the peace of the very elect, the most consecrated, most dedicated of God's children. To maintain unbroken peace in the face of assaults and attacks of this world, is nothing short of a miracle from heaven.

This is an age of speed and of nerves. The world rushes on in such haste as man has never known. Jesus said, "Man shall not live by bread alone—but by every word that proceedeth out of the mouth of God" (Matt. 4:4). In this age, man still cannot live "by bread alone" — but instead of supplementing his diet with Bread from heaven, he supplements with tranquilizers, aspirin, and vitamins that come in bottles!

What burdens men and women are carrying today! They have not stopped long enough to hear the Word of God saying, "Cast all your cares upon Him, for He careth for you!" Neither have they read, "I will never leave thee nor forsake thee, that we may boldly say, God is my helper and I shall not fear what man shall do unto me." In this hour of anxiety, high taxes (and many times, low wages), Psalm 37:25 would do more good than an aspirin tablet: "I have been young, and now am old; yet have I not seen the righteous forsaken, nor his seed begging bread!" Some of us who feel that we are persecuted, unappreciated and unwanted, should read, "I have learned in whatsoever state I am, therewith to be content" (Phil. 4:11). And then add, "If God be for us, who can be against us? We know that all things work together for good to them that love God, to them who are the called according to His purpose." These "spiritual vitamins" would do much more to tranquilize the spirit, mind and body than all the aspirin tablets in the world.

I am sure it is not easy to smile when the head of a family is out of work and the "income" does not match the "outgo." I am sure a wife becomes anxious when she tries desperately to help her husband make financial ends meet, and it is impossible to do so. In this age of nerves, when people are tired and worn, when many times they seemingly come to the breaking point, it is not easy to demonstrate "perfect peace." It is not easy — but it IS *possible* — because God's precious Word declares, "Thou wilt keep him in perfect peace whose mind is stayed on thee (Jesus)" (Isa. 26:3).

106

There are those who are lonely in soul, who feel that this world neither needs nor wants them. They feel they are of no use to anyone. Such despondency invites suicide. But the Word of God cries out, "Come unto Me . . . I will give you rest" (Matt. 11:28–30).

It is true that this age in which we are living is responsible for much of the anxiety and strain written on the faces of people as they rush pell-mell here and there; but the real trouble lies much deeper than the physical. The real trouble is in the heart. Most of us need to sit down before an open Bible and have a heart-to-heart talk with ourselves . . . with our God-given conscience. If we will be honest with ourselves, we will admit that a great deal of the trouble lies within us. We should ask ourselves some very pertinent questions – for instance: Why do we grow irritable? Why do our nerves get on edge, causing us to speak in haste and then only moments later regret every word we have said? Why do we "cross bridges before we come to them"? Why do we find it so difficult to relax and rest in Jesus? Why are there so many days when nothing seems to go right, everything goes wrong, our work is a burden and people around us are hard to live with? If we would take a little time to look into the mirror of our own life, we would have less time to criticize those around us. We might as well face the fact that we lack *the peace of Christ*—His last, most priceless gift to His children!

Yes, it is altogether possible to be born again—and yet not be a peacefully abiding child. "And now, little children, *abide in Him*; that, when He shall appear, we may have confidence, and not be ashamed before Him at His coming" (I John 2:28).

The devil holds over the heads of some of God's children the fact that they do not live as they should live, and therefore they may doubt that they have ever been saved. Jesus came to give life (John 10:10). He not only came to *give* life—but He came to give it *more abundantly*. Anything short of abundant life is taking God's second best. It is a sin to worry and fret. When Jesus, our Saviour, promised to supply our every need and go with us all the way—even unto the end—and to give us perfect peace, why should we worry? Why should we fret? Yet if we are honest, we must confess that we do.

Dear reader, would you like *peace* today? I do not mean the species of peace that would make one lazy and cause him to sit safe and sheltered, refusing to participate in life; I mean peace that brings calm and assurance in the midst of a troubled and troublesome world. I mean the peace that stands in the gateway of the soul and faces all manner of difficult things with steady eyes and steady hands—the peace that holds the heart serene and sweet through crowded days of overwork and criticism from those with whom you work, with whom you mix and mingle throughout the day. Would you like that kind of peace? You can have it—IF the Word of God is true — and God *cannot lie.*

This peace of which I speak is not a matter of temperament. It is available to the most highly strung, most explosive soul on earth. It is a matter of accepting the Lord Jesus Christ, the gift of God. HE is our peace: "MY PEACE I GIVE UNTO YOU."

In your heart and mind, please underline the two words, "MY PEACE." In other words, Jesus said, "I give unto you the peace that MY heart knows." Christ, who was rich, became poor for our sakes. For our sakes He stepped from the bosom of the Father to a manger in Bethlehem, into a world that hated Him and eventually nailed Him to a cross. He did not often speak about peace, but you can find the peace of God on every page in the Bible and in every chapter of every book from Genesis through Revelation.

Did anyone—even the enemies of Jesus—ever see Him irritated or fretted? As they watched His life He asked, "Which one of you convinceth me of sin?" Think what Jesus had to put up with! Could we have taken what He did, and remained serene and calm?

During His earthly stay there were continual intrusions upon His privacy. He was seldom alone in the hours between dawn and dusk. The steady, daily drain on His physical resources and strength was certainly far beyond anything we will ever experience. Inconsiderate people broke in upon His quiet hours. He was carrying the burden of the sins of the whole world. He was a man of sorrows and acquainted with grief. He was misunderstood, criticized and blasphemed. He was disappointed in His disciples. Yet, the crushing load of such a life did not cause Him to become irritable. Through it all He remained a calm, serene, untroubled person. He displayed no hurry and flurry, no strain, no trace of nerves. Whatever Jesus encountered, He was perfectly calm and serene. He did not find it necessary to run by the corner drug store two or three times a day for a headache powder and a tranquilizer.

Contrast the serenity of Jesus with the attitude of His disciples, whose nerves sometimes gave way — they were human. I love to study about Peter (I think I am closely related to Peter). In a Samaritan village the people were very rude and ugly, and the disciples cried out to Jesus, "Lord, let us call down fire from heaven! Let us teach these unlovable folks a lesson!" What did Jesus say? Jesus answered the disciples, "Ye know not what manner of spirit ye are of!"

109

One night a frail fishing boat was being tossed to and fro in a murderous storm at sea. The waves were boisterous, and it seemed that at any moment the little ship would fly into a thousand pieces. The disciples shouted, "MASTER! Do you not care that we perish? While we are about to be drowned, you are calmly sleeping!" What did Jesus do? He simply said, *"Peace . . . be still,"* and the angry waves became calm. I think He was speaking as much to the panic-stricken hearts of His disciples as to the stormy sea — and there is always an inner calm when Jesus speaks to our hearts.

On another occasion, five thousand people came out to hear Jesus preach. He spoke all day, and the people had been all day in the wilderness without food. I am sure some of them were very hungry. The disciples said, "Send them away"; but Jesus replied, "They need not depart. These are sheep without a shepherd. I love them, they are the people I came to save." Jesus never panicked. He was never irritable, even under such trying circumstances as having five thousand people to feed!

Then came the end, when Jesus set His face steadfastly toward Jerusalem, announcing every step of the way that He would be arrested, tried, condemned and crucified. The disciples fretted. They said, "Don't GO to Jerusalem." But the eye of Jesus was singled on Jerusalem, Calvary, the Cross. Then one night they went into the Garden of Gethsemane to pray, and when the enemy struck, the strained nerves of the disciples snapped completely. They fled. What did Jesus do? He stepped forward and calmly asked the officers whom they sought. When they said, "We seek Jesus of Nazareth," He replied, "I AM HE. If you have come for Jesus of Nazareth, then take me, and let my followers go." They arrested Jesus and took Him away, and all of the disciples deserted Him, save John—and

110

Peter (who followed afar off).

When they had beaten Jesus, mocked Him, plucked out His beard by the roots, spat in His face, they finally nailed Him to a cross. Through it all He was serene. His prayer was, "Father, forgive them, they know not what they do!" All the way from Bethlehem to Calvary, until He said, "Father, into thy hands I commend my spirit," Jesus had peace—strong, untroubled, undisturbed peace. That same peace can be yours and mine if we will fully and unreservedly surrender our all to the Prince of Peace.

No doubt someone is saying, "Mr. Greene, don't forget — that was Jesus, and I am not Jesus. He was different. I am but common clay, I am made of dust." I would be happy if, in this message, I could convince one troubled heart that this peace of Christ, the peace of God that passes all understanding, is not a far-off dream. THIS PEACE IS ACTUALLY WITHIN THE REACH OF ANYONE WHO WILL CLAIM IT. Remember, Jesus said, "It is MY peace"—and it is His gift to you!

But how does this peace come? How do we come into possession of Christ's peace? What is the secret? The answer is, "FAITH!" But what is *faith*? "Faith is the substance of things hoped for, the evidence of things not seen" (Heb. 12:1). The only way to possess the peace of Christ is to exercise faith *in* Christ. Simply say to yourself (and mean it), "Jesus took my place. He bore my sins in His body and nailed them to His cross. Jesus was tempted in all points as I am—yet was without sin. He did not have a home, a bed, a place to lay His head — yet He promised to supply all my needs. He is my Jesus, He is my Saviour. He said to me, 'Seek first the kingdom of God and His righteousness, and all these things shall be added unto you'" (Matt. 6:33).

Jesus cannot lie (Rom. 3:4; Heb. 6:18). So rest your

111

soul, your spirit, your body in His hands. By faith, believe that He saved you, by faith believe that He has forgiven your sins. By faith believe that your name is in the Lamb's Book of Life, and by faith believe that Jesus is able to keep you calm, collected and serene. Remember His promise, "Thou wilt keep him in perfect peace whose mind is stayed on Thee." Here and now, commit your mind, your soul, your body to Jesus; trust Him to give you the abundance of His grace.

Make yourself this promise: "This day I refuse to worry, knowing that all things work together for good to them that love God. I refuse to fret, knowing that if God be for me, who can be against me? I refuse to be anxious, knowing that not one sparrow falls to the ground but that God sees it. He knows the number of every hair in my head. Why should I fret? This day, I accept what Jesus bequeathed to me in His last will and testament. Here and now I accept by faith the peace of the Lord Jesus . . . peace that passeth all human understanding. Thank you, Jesus, that you said to me—yes, even to ME, 'Peace I leave with you, my peace I give unto you'" (John 14:27).

May God bless you and give you perfect peace.

THE MARK OF TRUE DISCIPLESHIP

THE MARK OF TRUE DISCIPLESHIP

"He that loveth father or mother more than me is not worthy of me: and he that loveth son or daughter more than me is not worthy of me. And he that taketh not his cross, and followeth after me, is not worthy of me" (Matt. 10:37,38).

Jesus declared that if we are not willing to forsake father, mother, brother, sister, houses and lands—and even our own life—we are not worthy to be His disciples. It might do most of us good to take stock of our spiritual standing with the Lord, and see if we are worthy disciples. Self-denial is foreign to many Christians. So many know nothing about denying self and bearing a cross for Jesus.

Jesus is our example. He was the most unselfish person ever to exist in this old universe — there was not a selfish deed or word throughout His entire ministry. Yet some who claim to be His followers are so selfish! One of the most inexcusable sins of Christianity is selfishness. Praise God, *salvation is free* — but "faith without works is dead."

In my mind's eye I can see a conference in heaven, six thousand years ago. Adam—God's perfect man—had sinned. The devil had robbed him of his first estate with a holy God. What could be done about it? That is what the conference was to decide. I see God the Father as He calls the Son—His ONLY Son—and the Holy Spirit, and tells them what has happened. It would be necessary for One to die, that man might escape eternal death in hell fire. I believe with all my heart that *without hesitation, Jesus said, "Father, I will go"*!

With the unselfishness of God, Jesus thought only of those who would be victims of the devil; He had no thought for Himself. He did not consider that His decision would cost Him:

His seat by the Father's side,
The presence of the face of the Father,
The glories of heaven,
The singing of the heavenly choir,
The worship He received from the heavenly hosts,
The streets of transparent gold.

Because of His unselfish love for mankind, He exchanged all this for:

Birth in a lowly stable,
Boyhood in a carpenter's shop,
Rejection by those He came to save,
The mocking and scourging He endured,
The cruel cross He was to bear,
The crown of thorns He was to wear,
The spikes through His hands and feet,
The mocking of the crowds as He died,
The forsaking by thousands He had blessed.

Yet many who claim to be His disciples have never made one single sacrifice for His name's sake!

Had Jesus been born into the home of a millionaire, His sacrifice would still have been beyond our comprehension. But He was not born to the wealth of this world. He was born in a stable, and I doubt not that He spent His childhood and youth helping Joseph in the little carpenter shop in Nazareth. He was God's only Son, the beloved of heaven; yet He left the Father's bosom and became the Son of a virgin, with a humble carpenter's home in which to dwell.

116

He sacrificed as a man. He lived the most sacrificial
life known to history. Every deed He did was for others.
In the street, by the seashore, in the boat . . . wherever
He went, He was doing deeds of kindness for those about
Him. Not one selfish deed could be charged against His
ministry. He healed the sick, gave sight to the blind,
restored the dead to life, gave hearing to the deaf, and
made the lame to walk. He cleansed the leper and fed
hungry thousands. On one occasion He said, "The foxes
have holes, and the birds of the air have nests—but the Son
of man hath not where to lay His head!" In a world made
by Him, He had no place to call His home.

Many times ministers of today feel that they must
have the best hotels in which to stay and the best of care
while they are in a city. Yet the Saviour they represent
had not "where to lay His head." God's picture of a
true minister of the Gospel is that of a humble servant. I
doubt not that many of the nights of Christ's public ministry were spent in the Garden of Gethsemane in prayer.

His sacrificial spirit followed Him to the end. After
the days of His public ministry had run their course and
when His hour had come, He was still the same unselfish
Saviour He had been all the way through. Having loved
His own, He loved them to the end. Knowing what lay
ahead of Him, He set His face toward Calvary, and no
enticement of Satan could turn Him aside. No disappointment could discourage Him. He had come into the world
to die for the sins of the world, that WE, through His
death, might live eternally.

In the Garden of Gethsemane, while His disciples
slept, Jesus prayed to the heavenly Father . . . a prayer
so fervent that His perspiration was as it were "great
drops of blood"! Before Him passed the cup that contained

your sins and mine—and not only OUR sins, but the sin
of the whole world—*past, present,* and *future.* What will H
do now—this Man who has *lived* for others and who now i
about to *die* for others?   In Matthew 26:38—45 we read
". . . My soul is exceeding sorrowful, even unto death . .
O my Father, if it be possible, let this cup pass from me
nevertheless not as I will, but as thou wilt.   Then H
cometh unto the disciples, and findeth them asleep, an
saith unto Peter, What, could ye not watch with me on
hour? . . . He went away again the second time, and prayed
saying, O my Father, if this cup may not pass away fro
me, except I drink it, thy will be done.   And He came an
found them asleep again: for their eyes were heavy.   An
He left them, and went away again, and prayed the thir
time, saying the same words.   Then cometh He to Hi
disciples, and saith unto them, Sleep on now, and tak
your rest: behold . . . the Son of man is betrayed into th
hands of sinners.''

Can you not hear the voice of Jesus as He praye
those words? "O, Father . . . *if it be possible . . .* !'' H
is saying to the Father, "If there be any other way t
save poor hell-bound souls of men, please provide it. B
if there is no other way except that I drink that cup . . .
will drink it!   Never mind my broken heart, my thorn
pierced brow, the plucking out of my beard by the root:
Never mind the Roman whipping post, the bleeding, tor
back.   Never mind that I must carry my own heavy cros
up Calvary's hill, that Roman spikes will pierce my hand
and feet.   Never mind the mocking crowd, the vinegar the
will give me to drink. Never mind that you, Father, wi
turn your head, and in the absence of your face I will cr
out, 'My God! My God! Why hast thou forsaken me!'   *If*
takes all that to keep sinners out of hell, I will drink th
cup to the last bitter dregs! THY WILL BE DONE!''

118

Only the Son of God could pray such an unselfish prayer as that. As I look over the years of my Christian life, I ask myself, What have I sacrificed for Him? What has it cost me to be a disciple? How does MY cross-bearing compare with His? What comparison can I make between what I have given up for Jesus, and what HE gave up for ME?

"If we suffer, we shall also reign with Him: if we deny Him, He also will deny us" (II Tim. 2:12). Have I suffered with Him? Have I sacrificed for Him? What has it cost me to be a disciple of the Lord? "He that findeth his life shall lose it: and he that loseth his life for My sake shall find it" (Matt. 10:39).

The world does not understand that kind of language. Unsaved people cannot understand it, because their minds are blinded by the devil—the god of this age. "The natural man receiveth not the things of the Spirit of God . . . because they are spiritually discerned" (I Cor. 2:14). Have I lost my life that I might find it again? Am I dead to self? Is Christ on the throne of my heart?

Jesus said, "Let him *deny himself . . . .*" What have I denied myself that I might be a better Christian? Do I always seek the comfort of myself before I decide to do a task for Jesus? When I feel led of the Lord to go and do His bidding, do I stop to see if it will be convenient for me? I am sure you have heard people say, "Don't do it if it will inconvenience you." Jesus said, "*Deny* yourself. Do the things for Me that cost you in personal comfort and convenience."

Jesus does not bind burdens upon His children. He does not make the road hard for us to travel; but when burdens come, He expects us to bear them like a good soldier of the cross. When the road is rough we are not

119

to turn back. "Take my yoke upon you, and learn of me...
For my yoke is easy, and my burden is light" (Matt. 11:
29,30). "Thou therefore endure hardness, as a good
soldier of Jesus Christ" (II Tim. 2:3). ". . . No man,
having put his hand to the plough, and looking back, is
fit for the kingdom of God" (Luke 9:62).

We have entirely too many fair-weather Christians.
One of the most tragic sights I know of is to see a church
on a real stormy Sunday morning, with about enough people present to fill the choir! The plant or place of business *next door to the church* will have every machine
running full blast on Monday morning, regardless of the
weather. I often feel like singing the old Negro Spiritual:
"Ever'body talkin' 'bout heaven ain't goin' there." Some
people serve God only when it is convenient, when it re-
quires no effort on their part, or when they have nothing
else to do. They are sunshine Christians . . . fair-weather
Christians.

I repeat — If we bear the cross, we shall share the
crown. If we deny the cross, we will have no part in the
crown. I want to have a part in the coronation, don't you?

I once read an article in the Christian Digest that
stirred my soul and made me feel *so small* in the sight of
God. Here it is:

"Bishop Francis Asbury, pioneer missionary to the
Indians, delivered 16,500 sermons, consecrated 4,000
preachers and covered 300,000 miles on horseback—a distance of twelve times around the earth. *He never had a
home, nor a bed of his own.*"

I thought of our missionaries around the world, many
of whom are sacrificing more than we on the home front
ever will. I have visited some of our foreign missions,
and I know what they are doing. When I was there I felt

120

so ashamed of myself for not having done more for missions and for the poor, unfortunate people who have never heard the wonderful story of Jesus and His love. It may well be that when the rewards are passed out in glory, we on the home field will be at the bottom of the list, while many dear missionaries who have sacrificed everything in this life to carry the Gospel will be rewarded a hundred-fold. Jesus is our Saviour; He is our example if we are true Christians. We should pray daily that God will help us to pattern our lives after Him.

He lived to die for your sins and mine. He does not require us to *die* for Him . . . He wants us to LIVE for Him—to present our bodies a living sacrifice, holy, acceptable unto Him, which is our reasonable service (Rom. 12:1).

Have you done that? Are you willing to follow Jesus? If you are a sinner, why not bow your head right now, and let the Lord Jesus come into your heart? If you have been a slothful Christian, why not consecrate your life to Him right now, and present to Him your very being as a living sacrifice, to be used of Him in whatever way will bring the greatest glory to His name? Do it now.

"PUT THAT ON MY ACCOUNT"

"PUT THAT ON MY ACCOUNT"

"If thou count me therefore a partner, receive him as yself. If he hath wronged thee, or oweth thee ought, put at on mine account" (Philemon 17 and 18).

These two verses, taken from the epistle of Paul to hilemon, give a perfect illustration of *imputation*. "Reeive him as myself. Philemon, reckon to Onesimus *my erit*; receive him as you would receive *me*. Think of him s you would think of me. If he has wronged you, if he wes you anything, put it on my account. Mark down his emerit to me, and put my merit to HIS credit. Give him edit for all good that you see in me, and put to my acount whatever he has done against you or whatever he wes you." *That is exactly what Jesus did for us:*

Our SIN was put to the account of Jesus:

We have all sinned and come short of the glory of God. here is none righteous, no, not one. There is not a just an upon the earth that doeth good and sinneth not. All e like sheep have gone astray.

In the Old Testament, God thundered out, "The soul at sinneth, it shall surely die!" In the New Testament e proclaims, "The wages of sin is death! When sin is nished, it bringeth forth death!" All men are in the same ategory, from the standpoint of being incapable of present-g themselves to God. Mankind is lost, doomed, and with-it hope. But Jesus took our place as having to do with -I-N.

"There is therefore *NOW no condemnation* to them hich are in Christ Jesus . . ." (Rom. 8:1). This suggests at up to the moment we ARE in Christ Jesus, condemna-on DOES rest upon us. But *why is condemnation lifted*?

125

"For the law of the Spirit of life in Christ Jesus hath made me *free* from the law of sin and death. For what the law could not do, in that it was weak through the flesh, God sending His own Son in the likeness of sinful flesh, and for sin, condemned sin in the flesh" (Rom. 8:2,3). (Notice the word "SIN"—singular; not "SINS"—plural.)

"That as sin hath reigned unto death, even so might grace reign through righteousness unto eternal life *by Jesus Christ our Lord*" (Rom. 5:21). *Sin* (singular) describes the Adamic nature — we are born in sin and shapen in iniquity. *Sins* (plural) are the fruits produced by the Adamic nature. Drinking, gambling, murder, adultery, lying, stealing — these things are the fruits of SIN.

"Therefore if any man be in Christ, he is a new creature: old things are passed away; behold, all things are become new. And all things are of God, who hath reconciled us to Himself by Jesus Christ, and hath given to us the ministry of reconciliation; To wit, that God was in Christ, reconciling the world unto Himself, not imputing their trespasses unto them; and hath committed unto us the word of reconciliation. Now then we are ambassadors for Christ, as though God did beseech you by us: we pray you in Christ's stead, be ye reconciled to God. For He (GOD) hath made Him (Jesus) to be sin for us (for you and me) who knew no sin (Jesus knew no sin); that we might be made the righteousness of God IN HIM" (II Cor. 5:17—21).

God put our sin to the account of Jesus. He made Jesus—the righteous, sinless One—to be sin for US, that in Him we might be saved from the penalty of sin: *eternal death!*

"Nor yet that He should offer Himself often, as the high priest entereth into the holy place every year with blood of others; for then must He often have suffered since the foundation of the world: BUT NOW ONCE IN THE

126

ND OF THE WORLD HATH HE APPEARED TO PUT
WAY SIN BY THE SACRIFICE OF HIMSELF" (Heb.
:25,26). Jesus came into this world on a singular mission:
'o bear sin, to take away sin, to satisfy God concerning
in—and to take the sinner's place. By the sacrifice of
Himself, Jesus put away SIN forever.

Sin is the transgression of God's law. Sin is over-
tepping the divine boundary between good and evil, be-
ween righteousness and unrighteousness. Sin is failing to
eet the divine standard. Sin is exercising self-will, re-
elling against divine authority. Sin is lawlessness and
nbelief. *"Whatsoever is not of FAITH is SIN."*

Sin is an act in which we violate the law of God and
efuse to be obedient to His revealed will. *Because* of
isobedience to God, unrighteousness is our plight; we are
ut of fellowship with God and we live in enmity toward
im. God has not changed His mind about sin, and until
ie sin-question is settled in Jesus, we dare not hope to
ee God.

In the first epistle of John we read, "That which we
ave seen and heard declare we unto you, that ye also may
ave fellowship with us: and truly our fellowship is with
ie Father, and with His Son Jesus Christ. And these
ings write we unto you, that your joy may be full. *This
en is the message which we have heard* of Him, and de-
lare unto you, that God is light, and in Him is no darkness
t all. If we say that we have fellowship with Him, and
alk in darkness, we lie, and do not the truth: But if we
alk in the light, as He is in the light, we have fellowship
ne with another, AND THE BLOOD OF JESUS CHRIST
IS SON CLEANSETH US FROM ALL SIN" (I John 1:3—7).

"THIS THEN IS THE MESSAGE:
God is light . . .
In Him is no darkness at all . . .

127

If we walk in the light (in God) . . .

The blood of Jesus Christ, God's Son, cleanseth us from all sin."

Notice that in every verse used thus far, the word is singular—SIN. The blood of Jesus Christ cleanses from ALL sin. It is SIN that condemns the sinner and damns the soul to an eternal hell.

In Galatians 2:20 Paul declares that he shared in the crucifixion of Jesus —that is, when Saul of Tarsus received Jesus in Damascus, he accepted everything that Jesus accomplished in His death: "I am crucified with Christ: nevertheless I live; yet not I, but Christ liveth in me: and the life which I now live in the flesh I live by the faith of the Son of God, who loved me, and gave Himself for me." Positionally, the believer is dead, "hid with Christ in God" (Col. 3:3).

The sinner, having believed on Jesus Christ, becomes a Christian — ". . . Christ in you, the hope of glory" (Col 1:27). In Christ we are complete: "For in Him dwelleth all the fulness of the Godhead bodily. *And ye are complete in Him*, which is the head of all principality and power" (Col. 2:9,10).

In the eternity behind us, the members of the Godhead had a divine conference and agreed that Jesus would be permitted to put our sins on His account. So He said to God the Father, "Whatever man has done to you, Father *put it on MY account!*" That is exactly what Jesus did when He willingly laid down His life that we might have eternal life through HIS shed blood.

"He that believeth on Him is not condemned: but he that believeth not is condemned already, because he hath not believed in the name of the only begotten Son of God" (John 3:18). A person need not commit but one sin to be damned forever — and that is *the sin of unbelief.* If he

128

believes not, he is condemned already, *"because he hath not believed* in the name of the only begotten Son of God."

2. Our SINS have been put to the account of Jesus:

The Lord Jesus not only died to save us from SIN — He died to also cleanse us from ALL SINS. He is seated today at the right hand of God the Father, to make intercession for us, and to plead our case (Heb. 1:1–3; I Tim. 2:5).

In I Corinthians 15:1–3 Paul said, "Moreover, brethren, I declare unto you the Gospel which I preached unto you, which also ye have received, and wherein ye stand; by which also ye are saved, if ye keep in memory what I preached unto you, unless ye have believed in vain. For I delivered unto you first of all that which I also received, how that Christ died for our sins according to the Scriptures."

To the Galatian Christians Paul said, "Grace be to you and peace from God the Father, and from our Lord Jesus Christ, who gave Himself for our sins, that He might deliver us from this present evil world, according to the will of God and our Father: To whom be glory for ever and ever. Amen" (Gal. 1:3–5). Notice the word *sins*. We know that Paul was writing to believers — those already saved from the penalty of unbelief; and he makes it very clear that Jesus not only gave Himself to redeem us from SIN, but also to deliver us from SINS.

One of the most touching verses in all of the Word of God is given to us through the inspired pen of Peter: "For even hereunto were ye called: because Christ also suffered for us, leaving us an example, that ye should follow His steps: Who did no sin, neither was guile found in His mouth: Who, when He was reviled, reviled not again; when He suffered, He threatened not; but committed Himself to Him that judgeth righteously: Who His own self bare our *sins* in His own body on the tree, that we, being dead to *sins*, should live unto righteousness: by whose stripes ye were healed" (I Pet. 2:21-24).

Notice that in this passage Peter said "SINS" (plural). Jesus not only paid the original *sin*-debt and bought the sinner back; He also paid for any other *sins* that may be committed. God Almighty has not changed His mind about sin. He still decrees, "The soul that sinneth shall die!" But Jesus took our place — and now God looks at the sinner through the blood of Jesus. Those who have trusted in His shed blood are just as pure as the blood that covers the believer's heart. "For Christ also hath once suffered for sins, the just for the unjust, that He might bring us to God, being put to death in the flesh, but quickened by the Spirit" (I Pet. 3:18).

In God's love-letter to His "little children," given to us through John the Beloved, we read, "My little children, these things write I unto you, that ye sin not. And if any man sin, we have an Advocate with the Father, Jesus Christ the righteous: And He is the propitiation for our *sins*: and not for our's only, but also *for the SINS of the whole world*" (I John 2:1,2).

These words are directed to God's "little children." There is no mistake as to whom the Holy Spirit is speaking: He is not speaking to unbelievers, but to God's born again ones. Jesus IS the propitiation for our sins—sins of omission and sins of commission. These sins have to do with the believer. *SIN damns* — but SINS rob us of power, joy, usefulness—and reward! "Herein is love, not that we loved God, but that He loved us, and sent His Son to be the propitiation for our SINS" (I John 4:10).

"And from Jesus Christ, who is the faithful witness, and the first begotten of the dead, and the prince of the kings of the earth. Unto Him that loved us, and washed us

130

from our SINS in His own blood, and hath made us kings
and priests unto God and His Father; to Him be glory and
dominion for ever and ever. Amen" (Rev. 1:5,6).

". . . He was wounded for our transgressions, He was
bruised for our iniquities: the chastisement of our peace
was upon Him; and with His stripes we are healed. All we
like sheep have gone astray; we have turned every one to
his own way; and the Lord hath laid on Him the iniquity of
us all" (Isa. 53:5,6).

"And their SINS and iniquities will I remember no
more" (Heb. 10:17).

There are people who say, "I would love to be a Christian if I only *knew* that I could live a Christian life." So
long as a person feels in his heart that he cannot live the
life of the Christian, the devil has that person exactly
where he wants him! It is impossible for the natural man,
in his own power, to live a Christian life. When God works
the miracle of grace in one's heart, and by faith in the
finished work of Jesus that person becomes a new creation,
he is made partaker of divine nature, he is indwelt by the
Holy Spirit, he will walk in the paths of righteousness for
Jesus' sake — and if that child of God *does* sin, the Saviour
is ready and anxiously waiting to propitiate to the Father.
Jesus took our place; He knows our life because He lived
on this earth just as we live—except without sin.

If you are not a believer, give your heart to Jesus
NOW. Take your Bible and read John 5:24, John 3:18,
Ephesians 2:8,9, Romans 10:9,10,13. Then bow your head
and in your own words tell God that you realize you are a
sinner, and on the basis of His Word ask Him to save you
for Jesus' sake. Invite Jesus to come into your heart—*and
He will.* Then turn in your Bible to I Corinthians 10:12,13
and memorize those two verses: "Wherefore let him that
thinketh he standeth take heed lest he fall. *There hath no*

temptation taken you but such as is common to man: bu
God is faithful, who will not suffer you to be tempted abov
that ye are able; but will with the temptation also make
way to escape, that ye may be able to bear it.''

Just remember that God is a million times more in
terested than YOU are in your living a victorious Christia
life, because when a born again child of God falls into sin
that child brings reproach upon the name of Jesus Christ
and God certainly does not want His children to disgrac
the name of His beloved Son. Therefore, the God who pro
vided redemption in Jesus and thus took care of SIN, als
made provision for SINS.

3. Our FAILURES were put to the account of Jesus:

"That which is born of the flesh is flesh; and tha
which is born of the Spirit is spirit" (John 3:6). Throug
the sin of Adam the entire human race was sold into si
and death, and since that day, flesh has produced n
better than sinful flesh. Because of Adam's sin, fles
could never have produced a Saviour. But Jesus took ou
failures, put them on His account, and bore them to th
cross that we might be born from above and become ne
creations in Christ Jesus, thus possessing divine nature.

In Matthew 7:16—18 Jesus said, "Ye shall know the
by their fruits. Do men gather grapes of thorns, or figs o
thistles? Even so every good tree bringeth forth good fruit
but a corrupt tree bringeth forth evil fruit. A good tree can
not bring forth evil fruit, neither can a corrupt tree brin
forth good fruit."

Because of Adam's sin, flesh is corrupt: "The hear
is deceitful above all things, and desperately wicked: wh
can know it?" (Jer. 17:9). From the unregenerate hear
proceed "evil thoughts, adulteries, fornications, murders
thefts, covetousness, wickedness, deceit, lasciviousness
an evil eye, blasphemy, pride, foolishness: All these evi

132

things come from within, and defile the man" (Mark 7:21-23).

It is from the heart that the issues of life proceed, and the unregenerate heart could never please God; but the failure of the first Adam was overcome by the success of the second Adam. Jesus was tempted in all points as we are, yet He was without sin. Read Matthew 4:1—11 and you will see that Jesus was tempted through every avenue employed by Satan to destroy a soul. Our Lord was tempted through the lust of the flesh, the lust of the eye, and the pride of life — but He was victorious over them all. He said, "Get thee hence, Satan: for it is written, Thou shalt worship the Lord thy God, and Him only shalt thou serve." And when the defeated tempter left Him, "angels came and ministered unto Him."

The Apostle Paul cried out, "Now if I do that I would not, it is no more I that do it, but sin that dwelleth in me" (Rom. 7:20).

John the Beloved said, "If we say that we have no sin, we deceive ourselves, and the truth is not in us" (I John 1:8).

The person who feels that he is good enough to go to heaven, that he does not need an old-fashioned mourner's bench, repentance, and blood-bought salvation, is deceiving no one but himself. We have all sinned, we are all sinners by nature; *and those who have not received Jesus by faith are sinners by choice*. The "perfectionist" who declares that he does not need a Saviour or the covering of the blood is deceived. In Bible language, he is a liar and the truth is not in him! Before an unbeliever can become a son of God he must admit the need of a Saviour. He must admit that he has sinned and come short of the glory of God, and that he rightfully deserves hell. He is then in a position to call on God for mercy — and God will forgive him and save him for Christ's sake.

133

Peter declared that he would never deny or forsake his Lord. But Jesus said, "Simon, Simon, behold, Satan hath desired to have you, that he may sift you as wheat: But I have prayed for thee, that thy faith fail not: and when thou art converted, strengthen thy brethren. And (Peter) said unto Him, Lord, I am ready to go with thee, both into prison, and to death. And He said, I tell thee, Peter, the cock shall not crow this day, before that thou shalt thrice deny that thou knowest me" (Luke 22:31—34). We know that Peter failed his Lord, we know that he repented and wept bitter tears of sorrow — and we know that Jesus forgave him. Yes, our *sin*, our *sins*, and our *failures* have been marked down to HIS account!

At the last Passover, Jesus girded Himself with a towel and began to wash the feet of His disciples. "Then cometh He to Simon Peter: and Peter saith unto Him, Lord dost thou wash my feet? Jesus answered and said unto him, What I do thou knowest not now; but thou shalt know hereafter. Peter saith unto Him, Thou shalt never wash my feet. Jesus answered him, *If I wash thee not, thou has no part with me*. Simon Peter saith unto Him, Lord, not my feet only, but also my hands and my head!" (John 13:6—9).

At that time, the disciples did not understand the meaning of what Jesus was doing. The "washing" went much further than simply rinsing away the dust of the road in Galilee: Jesus was presenting the divine truth that the needed washing—not in water—but *in the blood of the Lamb* "Without shedding of blood is no remission. . . The blood of Jesus Christ His Son cleanseth us from all sin" (Heb 9:22 and I John 1:7). Are YOU washed in the blood? If not, you are spiritually unclean and you cannot enter the City of God.

Paul said, "Wherefore He is able also to save them to the uttermost that come unto God by Him, seeing He

134

ever liveth to make intercession for them" (Heb. 7:25). Man is not able to save himself, he has failed God sadly and completely, and without the shed blood of Jesus there is no remission of sin. Without His confession to God the Father on our behalf, we could never see God (I Tim. 2:5). But because of His shed blood, God the Father can be just –and yet justify the ungodly:

"Being justified freely by His grace through the redemption that is in Christ Jesus: Whom God hath set forth to be a propitiation through faith in His blood, to declare His righteousness for the remission of sins that are past, through the forbearance of God; to declare, I say, at this time His righteousness: that He might be just, and the justifier of him which believeth in Jesus" (Rom. 3:24–26).

4. Our WEAKNESSES were put to the account of Jesus:

"Watch and pray, that ye enter not into temptation: The spirit indeed is willing, but the flesh is weak" (Matt. 26:41). Jesus spoke these solemn words to the disciples after finding them asleep. Who is he that overcometh but he that is born of the Spirit and washed in the blood? No flesh has ever been able to please God within itself. There must be One on the throne of the heart who is greater than the fleshly heart if we hope to please God. The spirit indeed is willing — but we live in a tabernacle of flesh that is exceedingly UNwilling to yield to the dictates of the Holy Spirit of God.

In I Thessalonians 5:17 Paul admonishes, *"Pray without ceasing."* To the believers in Rome he said, "Him that is weak in the faith receive ye, but not to doubtful disputations. For one believeth that he may eat all things: another, who is weak, eateth herbs. Let not him that eateth despise him that eateth not; and let not him which eateth not judge him that eateth: for God hath received him. Who art thou that judgest another man's servant? to his own

135

master he standeth or falleth. Yea, he shall be holden up: for God is able to make him stand" (Rom. 14:1—4).

We are not to sit in judgment against a fellow Christian who may stagger or stumble through some temptation that we have never had and about which we know nothing. In Paul's day some believers were quick to judge others who ate meat, and Paul rebuked them for this, admonishing them not to despise one another because they did not see eye to eye on secondary matters having to do with consecrated living. We are admonished in the Word of God, "Judge nothing before the time." We know that Jesus, the Righteous Judge, will judge *all things* in righteousness and we will receive justice and our true reward. It behooves us as individuals to be very careful to live clean, consecrated, dedicated lives, and to abstain from judging our fellow believers.

Jesus said, "Ye shall know them by their fruits." This means that those who drink, cheat, kill, lie, and live in open sin are certainly bearing the fruit of unrighteousness, and it is not judging to say that such a person is not a Christian. Certainly one who curses, lies, steals, gets drunk, gambles, and commits other such sins is bearing fruits of unbelief, not fruit of the Spirit:

". . . The fruit of the Spirit is love, joy, peace, longsuffering, gentleness, goodness, faith, meekness, temperance . . ." (Gal. 5:22,23). Those of us who are ministers, teachers—or even spiritually minded laymen—are instructed to "warn them that are unruly, comfort the feebleminded, support the weak, be patient toward all men" (I Thess. 5:14). We should warn other Christians who are stubborn, unruly, and high minded. We should never be harsh in dealing with a feebleminded person. We are to support those who are weak — we are to lift them up, not criticize them. When a weak brother stumbles, we who claim to be Christian are to lift him up, restore and strengthen him. Believers are to show patience toward "all men."

Paul had a thorn in the flesh, and he prayed for God to remove it. There has been much speculation as to what that thorn was (the Scriptures do not tell us), but regardless of what it was, God did not see fit to remove it. Paul said, "For this thing I besought the Lord thrice, that it might depart from me. And He said unto me, My grace is sufficient for thee: for *my strength is made perfect in weakness*. Most gladly therefore will I rather glory in my infirmities, that the power of Christ may rest upon me. Therefore I take pleasure in infirmities, in reproaches, in necessities, in persecutions, in distresses for Christ's sake: *for when I am weak, then am I strong*" (II Cor. 12:8–10).

Many times, we believers do not know when we really *are* strong. We do not realize when we are really rich or when we are really "on top." God's ways are not our ways. He knows best — and if He be for us, who can be against us? We know that all things work together for good to those who love God and are called according to His purpose. If we truly love God and know that He has called us into this life, we should not fret and worry, no matter what may come and go. We cannot lose if we know for sure "whom we have believed," for we should rest in confidence that HE is able!

In the eleventh chapter of Hebrews—that great roll-call of the faithful—we read of the men and women of great faith, many of whom are named there. And then we read, "And what shall I more say? For the time would fail me to tell of Gedeon, and of Barak, and of Samson, and of Jephthae; of David also, and Samuel, and of the prophets: Who through faith subdued kingdoms, wrought righteousness, obtained promises, stopped the mouths of lions, quenched the violence of fire, escaped the edge of the sword, OUT OF WEAKNESS WERE MADE STRONG, waxed valiant in fight, turned to flight the armies of the aliens. . . And these all, having obtained a good report through faith, received not the promise: God having provided some better thing for us, that they without us should not be made perfect" (Heb. 11:32–34, 39, 40).

God is no respecter of persons, and what He did for these dear souls—those who are named and the great army who are NOT named—He will do for you and for me. He put all of our weaknesses "on the account" of Jesus.

"Wherefore seeing we also are compassed about with so great a cloud of witnesses, let us lay aside every weight, and the sin which doth so easily beset us, and let us run with patience the race that is set before us, looking unto Jesus the author and finisher of our faith; who for the joy that was set before Him endured the cross, despising the shame, and is set down at the right hand of the throne of God" (Heb. 12:1,2).

5. God put all of our CARES on the account of Jesus:

"Humble yourselves therefore under the mighty hand of God, that He may exalt you in due time: Casting all your care upon Him; for He careth for you" (I Pet. 5:6,7). It grieves the heart of God when believers insist upon bearing their own burdens and cares. Jesus Christ bore our sin, our sins, our failures, our weaknesses — and it is His joy to bear our cares for us. He is just as concerned about us today as He was about His disciples, He loves us just as much as He loved them; and to those disciples He said:

"Take no thought for your life, what ye shall eat, or what ye shall drink; nor yet for your body, what ye shall put on. Is not the life more than meat, and the body than

138

raiment? Behold the fowls of the air: for they sow not, neither do they reap, nor gather into barns; yet your heavenly Father feedeth them. Are ye not much better than they? Which of you by taking thought can add one cubit unto his stature? And why take ye thought for raiment? Consider the lilies of the field, how they grow; they toil not, neither do they spin: And yet I say unto you, That even Solomon in all his glory was not arrayed like one of these. Wherefore, if God so clothe the grass of the field, which to day is, and to morrow is cast into the oven, shall He not much more clothe you, O ye of little faith? Therefore take no thought, saying, What shall we eat? or, What shall we drink? or, Wherewithal shall we be clothed? (For after all these things do the Gentiles seek:) for your heavenly Father knoweth that ye have need of all these things. But seek ye first the kingdom of God, and His righteousness; and all these things shall be added unto you. Take therefore no thought for the morrow: for the morrow shall take thought for the things of itself. Sufficient unto the day is the evil thereof" (Matt. 6:25—34).

Since Jesus Christ cares for the lilies, the sparrows, the grass of the fields, surely He will take care of His born again ones. What a happy day it will be for believers when we learn with Paul, in whatsoever state we find ourselves, therein to be content! It is a sin to worry, to be anxious, to fret about "things" when we know the God who created ALL things, and who is able to supply our every need!

Jesus loved to visit in the home of Mary, Martha, and Lazarus. They made Him welcome, and He found kindred spirits there, from the human standpoint, which were not found in every home He visited. In that home one day, a very interesting thing happened: ''Now it came to pass, as they went, that He entered into a certain village: and a certain woman named Martha received Him into her house. And she had a sister called Mary, which also sat at Jesus' feet, and heard His Word. But Martha was cumbered about

139

much serving, and came to Him, and said, Lord, dost thou not care that my sister hath left me to serve alone? Bid her therefore that she help me. And Jesus answered and said unto her, Martha, Martha, thou art careful and troubled about many things: But one thing is needful: and Mary hath chosen that good part, which shall not be taken away from her" (Luke 10:38—42).

In a kind, sweet and humble way, Jesus rebuked Martha for being cumbered about much serving, when she could have been sitting at His feet! This was the same Lord who took the few loaves and fishes and fed five thousand. It would have been but a small matter for Him to have fed Mary and Martha—both spiritually AND physically; but Martha was disturbed about the dinner which she must prepare and serve that night.

"And seek not ye what ye shall eat, or what ye shall drink, neither be ye of doubtful mind" (Luke 12:29).

To the believers at Philippi Paul gave this wonderful advice: "Let your moderation be known unto all men. The Lord is at hand. Be careful for nothing; *but in every thing by prayer and supplication with thanksgiving let your requests be made known unto God.* And the peace of God, which passeth all understanding, shall keep your hearts and minds through Christ Jesus" (Phil. 4:5—7).

If you are bearing your own cares, if the cares of this life trouble and torment you, robbing you of your spiritual birthright of peace, contentment, joy unspeakable and full of glory, it is not God's fault — it is your own fault. God made provision for our cares in Jesus Christ: They have all been put to His account.

6.   Our SORROWS have been put on the account of Jesus:

Man born of woman is of few days and full of trouble. Sorrow began in the Garden of Eden. Tears have flowed from the eyes of mortal man ever since the day of Adam's sin. Rivers of tears have been shed by brokenhearted mothers and fathers, husbands and wives, sons and daughters. Both young and old face sorrows; but the all-sufficient One has taken care of our sorrows. He was definitely a man of sorrows. He was acquainted with grief. ". . . And we hid as it were our faces from Him; He was despised, and we esteemed Him not. Surely He hath borne our griefs, and carried our sorrows: Yet we did esteem Him stricken, smitten of God, and afflicted. But He was wounded for our transgressions, He was bruised for our iniquities: the chastisement of our peace was upon Him; and with His stripes we are healed. . . He was oppressed, and He was afflicted, yet He opened not His mouth: He is brought as a lamb to the slaughter, and as a sheep before her shearers is dumb, so He openeth not His mouth" (Isa. 53:3–7).

Concerning Israel, God said, ". . . I have surely seen the affliction of my people which are in Egypt, and have heard their cry by reason of their taskmasters; for I know their sorrows" (Ex. 3:7). The God of Israel is OUR God. Not one tear has fallen from the eye of a believer without the knowledge of God Almighty and Jesus Christ our Saviour. It is comforting to know that the Saviour whom we know, love, and serve, shed tears when He walked this earth. He wept at the tomb of Lazarus, and He wept over the Holy City Jerusalem. He was a man of sorrows, a man of tears. He was acquainted with grief, and He tasted sorrow for us, that WE, in the midst of tears and sorrow, might be able to rejoice, knowing that we are on the victory side. If God be for us, we cannot, we shall not, lose the battle!

The touching significance of the book of Lamentations lies in the fact that in that book we find the disclosure of the love and sorrow of Jehovah God for His chosen people

141

whom He was forced to chasten because of their sin. In Lamentations 1:12 Jeremiah cries out, "Is it nothing to you, all ye that pass by? Behold, and see if there be any sorrow like unto my sorrow, which is done unto me, wherewith the Lord hath afflicted me in the day of His fierce anger!"

The sorrow of Jehovah over His people burned in the very bones and heart of Jeremiah: "But if ye will not hear it, my soul shall weep in secret places for your pride; and mine eye shall weep sore, and run down with tears, because the Lord's flock is carried away captive" (Jer. 13:17).

It is the good pleasure of God to withhold no good thing from them who walk uprightly — but He chastens those who refuse to obey His will. Paul warned the Corinthian believers that if they had judged themselves, they would not have been judged; but because of their actions and conduct in the church, many were weak, others were sick— and some were dead. God is a God of sorrow. Jesus bore OUR sorrows while He was here upon earth, He nailed them to His cross, and if we continue to carry our own sorrow, it is our fault—not His.

7.   Our DEATH was put on the account of Jesus:

God said, "The soul that sinneth, it shall surely die." Jesus said, "Put that on MY account." In spite of the fact that more books have been written about Jesus Christ than about any other person who ever lived, He came into this world on a singular mission: *To satisfy the heart of God concerning the sin question and the sinner.* God created man in His own image, and He did not create him to be destroyed and damned! Man was created for God's own pleasure and joy; he was created to honor and worship God. But Adam deliberately disobeyed God, he sinned, and God had no alternative but to carry out the sentence. He had

142

clearly warned Adam, "The day you eat thereof, you shall surely die." He cannot, and He does not, change His mind.

But Jesus put death to HIS account and took our place: He died for us.

". . . What is man, that thou art mindful of him? or the son of man, that thou visitest him? Thou madest him a little lower than the angels; thou crownedst him with glory and honour, and didst set him over the works of thy hands. . . . *But we see JESUS, who was made a little lower than the angels FOR THE SUFFERING OF DEATH, crowned with glory and honour; THAT HE BY THE GRACE OF GOD SHOULD TASTE DEATH FOR EVERY MAN.* . . Forasmuch then as the children are partakers of flesh and blood, He also Himself likewise took part of the same; that through death He might destroy him that had the power of death, that is, the devil; and deliver them who through fear of death were all their lifetime subject to bondage" (Heb. 2:6–15 in part).

Jesus said, "I am the resurrection, and the life: he that believeth in me, though he were dead, yet shall he live: And whosoever liveth and believeth in me shall never die" (John 11:25,26).

". . . When this corruptible shall have put on incorruption, and this mortal shall have put on immortality, then shall be brought to pass the saying that is written, Death is swallowed up in victory. O death, where is thy sting? O grave, where is thy victory? The sting of death is sin; and the strength of sin is the law. But thanks be to God, which giveth us the victory through our Lord Jesus Christ" (I Cor. 15:54–57).

"For the Lord Himself shall descend from heaven with a shout, with the voice of the archangel, and with the trump of God: and the dead in Christ shall rise first: Then we which are alive and remain shall be caught up together

143

with them in the clouds, to meet the Lord in the air: and so shall we ever be with the Lord" (I Thess. 4:16,17).

". . . Truly as the Lord liveth, and as thy soul liveth, *there is but a step* between me and death!" (I Sam. 20:3b).

Death is a Bible fact to which graveyards, undertakers, and tombstone makers testify. And since no one has been able to prove that there is no hereafter and no life after death, since no one has been able to prove that there is no heaven or hell, does it not seem reasonable that we should prepare for the other side of the grave?

As for me and my house, I believe exactly what the Bible teaches about life after death. I also believe that "it is appointed unto men once to die, but after this the judgment" (Heb. 9:27). I believe this solemn Bible fact, and I have obeyed the admonition, "Prepare to meet thy God." I am saved by the grace of God, my sins are under the blood. Jesus my Saviour said, "Whatever sin Oliver Greene has committed, or may commit; all of his failures, his weaknesses, his cares and sorrows—and the death he should die in hell because of his sin—PUT THEM ALL TO MY ACCOUNT!" I have personally received Jesus as my Saviour. I do not desire to die, but I am not afraid to die! It does not frighten me to face the fact that there is but a step between me and death.

What about YOU, dear reader? If you are not saved, call on God this very moment. "Believe on the Lord Jesus Christ, and thou shalt be saved" (Acts 16:31). Receive Him — and He will immediately make you His son.

"But as many as received Him, to them gave He power to become the sons of God, even to them that believe on His name: Which were born, not of blood, nor of the will of the flesh, nor of the will of man, but of God" (John 1: 12,13).

"That if thou shalt confess with thy mouth the Lord

144

Jesus, and shalt believe in thine heart that God hath raised Him from the dead, thou shalt be saved. For with the heart man believeth unto righteousness; and with the mouth confession is made unto salvation" (Rom. 10:9,10).

"For by grace are ye saved through faith; and that not of yourselves: it is the gift of God: Not of works, lest any man should boast" (Eph. 2:8,9).

GOD'S HEROES

GOD'S HEROES

Limited time and space will not permit us to print our entire text here; so before reading this message, please read the eleventh chapter of Hebrews and note every verse carefully. Spiritual heroism is demonstrated through five elements, and in this chapter of Hebrews these five elements are manifested in the lives of God's heroes of the days before the coming of the Lord Jesus to pay sin's debt in full:

1. Sacrifice: This element is demonstrated in the life of Abel. "By faith Abel offered unto God a more excellent sacrifice than Cain, by which he obtained witness that he was righteous, God testifying of his gifts: and by it he being dead yet speaketh" (Heb. 11:4).

It does not take a hero to receive FROM God; there is no demonstration of heroism in receiving the bountiful blessings God gives to His children in answer to prayer. Even the weakest saint can receive from God in answer to sincere prayer from the heart: but Abel "OFFERED UNTO GOD." It matters not how humble the service performed by a believer unto God, that service is noted. One great artist of the past painted an outstanding picture in which he represented angels as servants in the kitchen, helping a tired mother with plain domestic duties.

An old blacksmith, while making sparks fly from his anvil, was asked, "Sir, just what are you doing?" He replied, "I am preaching the Gospel to the heathen beyond. I am making a shoe for the horse used by our missionaries!" He was performing a very humble task—just the simple shaping of a horseshoe from crude iron — but he was truly preaching the Gospel to the heathen to whom the missionary would minister.

God has a great host of children who are continually asking—as indeed He wants us to do: "*Ask*, and ye shall receive." But we are also commanded to *give*. Paul said, "I beseech you therefore, brethren, by the mercies of God, that ye present your bodies a living sacrifice, holy, acceptable unto God, which is your reasonable service" (Rom. 12:1). God takes great pleasure in giving, but He also has great joy in receiving—especially an offering such as Abel gave.

Abel's offering was acceptable to God because it was according to God's plan for the forgiveness of sins. Undoubtedly the desire of Abel's heart was to be rid of sin; therefore he came to God with a blood offering—a lamb—thus pointing to "the Lamb of God, which taketh away the sin of the world" (John 1:29). On the other hand, Cain—like the Pharisee who prayed unto himself in Luke 18—offered a bloodless sacrifice. He offered unto God the fruits of the fields.

I do not doubt that Cain offered the *best* fruit — but the one thing he forgot was that God is not looking for a *beautiful* sacrifice, but a sacrifice of blood: "Without shedding of blood is no remission" (Heb. 9:22). If Cain really believed that he was a sinner and needed forgiveness of sins, he also believed (as demonstrated by his actions) that his labor, his wisdom, and the product of his own works was good enough! If God wanted an offering, He could take what Cain gave — and if that offering were not sufficient, he certainly would not bring another. That was the spirit he manifested when God said, "You have done wrong; but if you will do well, you will be accepted."

We know that Cain did not obey God; and Scripture records that a short time later while in the field with Abel, he grew angry with his brother and murdered him, because

150

Abel offered unto God a sacrifice well pleasing — not because he was a better boy than Cain, but because he offered a blood offering.

Our text records that Abel, "being dead, yet speaketh." That is, real self-sacrifice never dies. Men who give themselves in sacrifice to God, serving mankind while serving God, are never forgotten. To their fellowman, they are heroes. But *why did Abel offer a lamb?* The answer is in Hebrews 11:4: "BY FAITH." The only way to obtain faith that would bring obedience to God is by hearing the Word. God commanded Abel, and Abel acted in accordance with that command. God is no respecter of persons; He gave Cain the same message He gave Abel, and then went the "second mile" and *gave Cain a second chance*. But in spite of the longsuffering of God, Cain refused to be obedient and bring the sacrifice God demanded. Read the story in Genesis 4:1–13.

2. Persistent, consecrated, Christian living, under all circumstances: This element of spiritual heroism was set forth in the life of Enoch, who lived in one of the darkest days of human history, just before the flood: "By faith Enoch was translated that he should not see death; and was not found, because God had translated him: for before his translation he had this testimony, that he pleased God" (Heb. 11:5).

There were few men in Enoch's day who either feared or respected God, but Enoch walked with Him. (Please note that he did not beg God to walk with *him*—but he simply fell in step with God and came alongside Him in the yoke.) Jesus said, "Take my yoke upon you . . . come with me side by side, and we will walk together."

Any ordinary Christian can walk with God while in company with others who walk with Him; but it takes a real spiritual hero to say "No" when everyone else says

"Yes," or turn to the right when everybody else turns to the left — to walk with God when all others are walking with Satan. Enoch did just that. Too many of us exhaust our spiritual strength begging God to walk with *us*, *agree* with us and come to our assistance, when what we need is to get in step with God and walk with HIM.

The story is told that President Abraham Lincoln set aside a day of fasting and prayer, that God might be on the side of the Union; but a humble soldier in Lincoln's army said to him, "Do not bother about praying that God will get on OUR side; what we need to do is get on GOD'S side." That is true; for God is on the right side, God is righteous, He cannot BE wrong nor DO wrong. We need to be like Enoch and walk with God, come along in step with Him, for He is always in the right path. We may be in the minority, but if we are walking with God we are always in the majority — and that pays great dividends in the end.

Enoch was extraordinary — *he was a hero every day.* He walked patiently, persistently, continually and untiringly with God. It is not too difficult to walk with God on special occasions, but Enoch was not that kind of Christian — *he* walked with God *daily*. "They that wait upon the Lord shall renew their strength; they shall mount up with wings as eagles; they shall run, and not be weary; and they shall walk, and not faint" (Isaiah 40:31).

It is easy to be a hero on special occasions when the eyes of the world are upon you. Elijah was a hero on Mount Carmel—but that same Elijah whimpered under the juniper tree. It is much harder to be a hero under a juniper than on Mount Carmel or when the multitudes are falling at our feet declaring what a great person we are. Jonah was a hero at Nineveh — but a little later he sat under a gourd vine begging God to let him die!

Enoch was not that kind of hero. So far as we know, Enoch never complained about the gross wickedness and multitudes of ungodly men around him. He walked with God even though he walked alone so far as men were concerned. He walked with God while the multitudes walked FROM God in exactly the opposite direction. It is easy to go along with the crowd, floating downstream, as it were; but when the crowd turns against you, it is not so easy to walk step by step with God. True spiritual heroism consists in walking with God moment by moment, day by day, month by month and year by year. Enoch did just that — "and God took him!"

3. Fear: This element of spiritual heroism was manifested in the life of Noah. "By faith Noah, being warned of God of things not seen as yet, *moved with fear*, prepared an ark to the saving of his house; by the which he condemned the world, and became heir of the righteousness which is by faith" (Heb. 11:7).

"Fear makes cowards—or heroes." The *fear of God* makes a believer a spiritual hero; the fear of *man* makes him a coward. Fear to do *wrong* makes a believer a spiritual hero; fear to do *right* makes him a coward. God warned Noah of things "not seen as yet." Noah had never seen a drop of rain, for until he finished the ark and entered it, it had never rained. Until the flood, a mist had risen from the ground and watered the earth. But God said, "Noah, I am going to send a flood. You build an ark, and build it according to my directions." Even though Noah had never seen a flood (nor had he ever seen an ark) *he believed God*.

Noah might have presented scores of arguments against a flood; but since God said there would BE a flood, His word to Noah was stronger than any argument, and he immediately began to build an ark. There is a great need for a healthy fear of God among believers today. Thank

God for Calvary with its whisperings of the tender love of God and the longsuffering of the Lamb who shed His blood for the remission of sin; but we need to hear the thundering of Sinai. We need to preach the love of God — but we also need to declare that "our God is a consuming fire." We need to preach that there is a Paradise in which believers rest — but we also need to preach that there is a burning hell where *unbelievers* will spend eternity begging for a drop of water to cool their parching tongues.

Noah was moved by fear. If there was to be a flood, if the earth was to be covered with water, that was frightening — but *since God said it*, Noah *believed* it; and moved with fear, he built the ark and saved his house, thereby condemning the world and becoming the heir of the righteousness which is by faith. It all happened because Noah believed God — and believing God produces the fear of God.

Believers today should fear God in that we are afraid to do what He commands us NOT to do, and we should be afraid to leave undone what He commands us to do. That is the kind of fear that makes spiritual heroes. We are not to be afraid of God in the same way we would fear a man-eating tiger, but we should fear Him with reverence—the same way in which our children fear us if we are the kind of parents we should be.

Do you fear God? Have you heard His Word as having to do with your work in bringing men to Jesus, thus testifying against the world? God does not want you to build an ark . . . *He wants you to be a witness*. He wants you to be afraid NOT to witness, because Jesus said, "Go ye into all the world and make disciples." Our command in this day is not to build an ark—but to "preach the Word, be instant in season, out of season." Tell men the sin-debt has been paid. Ask them, "What think ye of Christ?

Whose Son is He?" You and I should be afraid *not* to witness — and by like token we should fear to do those things God commands us *not* to do, for God plants in our hearts the brand of godly fear shown forth by Noah.

4. Obedience: This element was demonstrated in the life of Abraham. "By faith Abraham, when he was called to go out into a place which he should after receive for an inheritance, obeyed: and he went out, not knowing whither he went. . . By faith Abraham, when he was tried, offered up Isaac: and he that had received the promises offered up his only begotten son. Of whom it was said, That in Isaac shall thy seed be called: accounting that God was able to raise him up, even from the dead; from whence also he received him in a figure" (Heb. 11:8,17-19).

Abraham obeyed God in spite of God's former promise to him that in Isaac all the nations of the earth should be blessed; therefore in Abraham's case there was a direct conflict between the *command* of God and the *promise* of God. But in spite of the way it might seem in the light of human reasoning, *Abraham believed God.* He believed the promise; and as he was preparing to obey God's command ("esteeming that God was able to raise up Isaac from the dead"), he was, in his heart, *believing, knowing,* and *trusting* that God would work it out. As Abraham walked up the slopes of Mount Moriah, as he bound Isaac and laid him on the altar, he was sure that he was obeying God—and not hindering God's fulfillment of the promise that in Isaac all nations of the earth should be blessed. Please read Genesis 12.

Even while Isaac lay bound upon the altar, Abraham knew that he would take his only son back to Sarah that night—whole and in perfect health. He knew it would take a miracle to do it — but *he believed in the God of miracles*!

155

He believed that God would keep His promise if he (Abraham) obeyed God's command.

You and I must obey the command of God if we hope for God to fulfill His promises to us. God does not *suggest* that we repent — we are *commanded* to do so (Luke 13:3,5). God does not *suggest* that we be born again — we are *commanded* to be born again: "Except a man be born again, he cannot enter into the kingdom of God" (John 3:1–7). If we surrender soul, spirit and body to Jesus, if we walk in the light as He is in the light, no good thing will He withhold from us; but if we refuse to obey His commands we cannot expect to receive the promises.

It matters not whether we fully understand the way He leads and the things we are called upon to do. We are not commanded to *understand* . . . we are commanded to *obey*. Jesus said to His disciples, "Have faith in God" (Mark 11:22). If we believe in God—the God who must always do right simply because He IS God; if we believe as Abraham believed God, we will demonstrate the spirit of heroism such as Abraham demonstrated when he took his child, bound him, laid him on the altar and raised the knife. Then God worked a miracle. (God's miracles always follow personal, complete obedience to His command.) "Abraham believed God, and it was imputed unto him for righteousness." Please study carefully Romans chapter 4 in its entirety.

Yes, even though Abraham was a hundred years old, and Sarah, his dear wife, was also past the age of childbearing, and from the standpoint of mortal reasoning there could be no children — *Abraham believed God* that Isaac would be born. *After* Isaac was born and God commanded him to take the boy and offer him as a sacrifice (which seemed to be God working against Himself), Abraham

156

believed God, although he did not understand. He obeyed—
and won for himself the name "the friend of God." My
prayer is, "Oh, God, help me to obey as faithful Abraham
obeyed."

5. Self-denial: This element was demonstrated in the
life of Moses. "By faith Moses, when he was born, was
hid three months of his parents, because they saw he was
a proper child; and they were not afraid of the king's commandment. By faith Moses, when he was come to years,
refused to be called the son of Pharaoh's daughter; choosing rather to suffer affliction with the people of God, than
to enjoy the pleasures of sin for a season; esteeming the
reproach of Christ greater riches than the treasures in
Egypt: for he had respect unto the recompense of the reward. By faith he forsook Egypt, not fearing the wrath of
the king: for he endured, as seeing Him who is invisible"
(Heb. 11:23–27).

I suppose no person ever turned his back on more than
did Moses. The king offered him everything that one mortal
could offer another; but Moses BY FAITH turned it down!
He refused to be called the son of Pharaoh's daughter,
which would make him the grandson of the king, and chose
rather to suffer with God's people. He counted the reproach of Christ greater riches than the silver, gold, and
jewels of Egypt. We need more believers in our churches
today with the spirit of self-denial demonstrated by Moses
in the courts of Pharaoh.

Many times it is much more heroic to refuse than to
offer; more heroic to persist in fear of and obedience to
God, rather than yield to the glitter of the world's gold
and the glamor and pleasures of mankind. To be sure,
wealth, pleasure, honor, and position are enticing and
alluring to a youthful mind. All of these were offered to

157

Moses — but there was a condition attached: *Moses must link himself with the family of Pharaoh.* He refused — and by so doing demonstrated the self-denial that makes one a spiritual hero, and at the end of life's journey brings "a full reward" (II John 8).

Sin brings pleasures — and sin's pleasures are very attractive. America today needs some of the puritanism that caused believers to refuse to indulge in things of the world and link themselves with ungodly people or evil institutions. We need believers with a backbone—with a will and determination—who, like Daniel, will purpose in their hearts not to defile themselves. We need believers who will say to the world, "I do not dance, I do not play cards, I do not attend worldly affairs, I do not drink wine, beer or liquor, and I do not gamble — because to do any of these things would link me to the world with its evil institutions and evil people. If I indulge in these pleasures I become a symbol of evil—not of righteousness; and when people see me they will not think of God, but will rather be reminded of Egypt or of Sodom!" In this day of Laodicean living, Christian liberty is being brutally abused.

I John 2:15—17 commands us, *"Love not the world, neither the things that are in the world.* If any man love the world, the love of the Father is not in him. For all that is in the world, the lust of the flesh, and the lust of the eyes, and the pride of life, is not of the Father, but is of the world. And the world passeth away, and the lust thereof: but he that doeth the will of God abideth for ever!"

There are many things a believer can do and not burn in hell for doing them: but if he practices questionable habits and pleasures, he will lose his reward and by so doing may cause some weak one to stumble into hell. Paul said to those to whom he preached in his day, "I have a right to eat meat offered to idols; but if eating this meat causes a weaker brother to stumble, I will eat no flesh while the world stands, lest I make my brother to offend." There is nothing more heroic than the spirit which leads a believer to surrender all — even those things that may be harmless to him . . . the spirit that says with Paul, "If eating meat causes a weaker one to stumble, then I will eat no meat. If the pleasure I enjoy causes one to stumble, then I will yield my pleasure to God. I will eat, drink, and do whatsoever I do to the glory of God."

God help me to make this my daily prayer: "Wherever I go, whatever I do, whatever I say, whatever I am, may I always note that God is looking, listening, and Heaven keeps books."

Faith is the basis of all spiritual character. Love, hope, humility, joy — all wither and fade into insignificance without true faith. True faith comes only by hearing, and hearing by the Word of God (Rom. 10:17). Faith is the root from which grow the fruits of Christian living, Christian character and Christian heroism. To him who believes — as did Abel, Enoch, Noah, Abraham and Moses — ALL THINGS ARE POSSIBLE!

Dear believer, have faith in God — and all else will take care of itself. Jesus said it in these words: "Seek ye first the kingdom of God, and His righteousness; and all these things shall be added unto you" (Matt. 6:33).

WORD FROM OUTER SPACE

WORD FROM OUTER SPACE

"In the beginning was the Word, and the Word was with God, and the Word was God. The same was in the beginning with God" (John 1:1,2).

In these days we hear much about "outer space." Millions of dollars have been spent — and *billions* WILL BE spent if Jesus tarries — in man's attempt to probe outer space, reach the moon and perhaps go even further! Only God knows what is in the minds of some men.

We truly have mental giants on earth today. *Thinking* people admit that much progress has been made in man's attempt to discover what lies beyond the atmosphere of this earth. In this message I want to discuss "word from outer space," and word that will come *again* from outer space.

I.

In John's Gospel, chapter 1, verses 1 through 18, we have a marvelous description of the Word. John loved to refer to Christ as "The Word." (He is the only apostle who referred to the Lord in that way.) John was assured that Jesus was the Word, that He fully expressed GOD in word, and to John the Beloved the Holy Spirit dictated five of the New Testament books.

On three different occasions John speaks of The Word:

"In the beginning was the Word, and the Word was with God, and the Word was God. . . And the Word was made flesh, and dwelt among us . . . No man hath seen God at any time; the only begotten Son, which is in the bosom of the Father, He hath declared Him" (John 1:1,14,18).

God the eternal Spirit has always been — there was never a time when He was not (Psalm 90:1,2). He is no longer the inscrutable One. He is no longer the remote, far-away Person many think Him to be. God has been expressed in the Person of the Son of His love, the Lord Jesus Christ. Jesus wrapped God up in flesh, brought Him down to man, and declared Him. Words declare *who* we are and *what* we are. If we listen long enough to the conversation of a person, words will clearly tell us what is in the mind and heart of that person.

Jesus left the bosom of the Father and came into this world in a body of flesh. He did not take the form of an angel, but the form of sinful man, that He might taste death for every man and destroy him who had the power of death, the devil (Heb. 2:9,14,15).

Jesus was the Word; and when He came upon the scene of His public ministry He made a declaration concerning God. In all the Bible there is no verse that better tells us what Jesus declared, than John 3:16: "For God so loved the world, that He gave His only begotten Son, that whosoever believeth in Him should not perish, but have everlasting life!"

A. Jesus declared, *"God loves."* When we hear the thunder of Sinai and see the lightning as it splits the sky, we think of God as a consuming fire; but when we hear Jesus speak of the Father, He speaks in tender words: "God so loved." What a thrilling, comforting, assuring declaration!

B. Jesus declared that God not only loved, but that He did something to prove His love: *"God gave."* The Word was made flesh, took a body and tabernacled among us, "and we beheld His glory . . . full of grace and truth." Grace saves us, and truth sets us free. Jesus humbled Himself and became obedient unto death—even the death of the cross. He was rich with the Father, He dwelt in the riches of heaven — yet He became poor that we, through His poverty, might be made rich. God so loved, He gave His only begotten Son.

C. Jesus declared that God not only loved and not only gave, but *"God offers"* to any and all. Jesus expressed it in these words: "That whosoever believeth in Him should not perish, but have everlasting life!" This declaration goes beyond anything the Jewish rabbis ever taught or said. In the beginning it was clearly fixed in the mind of God that man should share His life in eternity—that is, all men who believe on Jesus and trust in the shed blood of His cross. In the beginning, before God laid the foundation of this world, it was foreordained that the Lamb of God would pay the sin-debt in order that man could be made partaker of divine nature. This was all decided before ever the world was made, and it would have remained an eternal secret had not God declared it in the Son, through the Word.

The first word that came from outer space was the Word of God, wrapped up in flesh, brought down to man to declare God's love, God's gift, and God's offer to all who will believe and receive the finished work of the Lord Jesus.

II.

The Word that was in the bosom of the Father, who in a body of flesh came from outer space into this world and declared the Father, after this mission was completed *returned TO the Father:*

"For there are three that bear record in heaven, the Father, the Word, and the Holy Ghost: and these three are one" (I John 5:7). Even in John's day, false teachers had already come upon the scene. In I John 4:1 we are warned to try the spirits, whether they be of God. There were those who were teaching error, mixing law and grace, adding tradition; but John declares that the record is settled and secure in heaven, and the three who bear record are

165

the Father, the Word, the Holy Ghost.

In this verse we have the truth, the witness, the record. What IS the record? It is declared in these words: "And this is the record, that God hath given to us eternal life, and this life is in His Son. He that hath the Son hath life; and he that hath not the Son of God hath not life" (I John 5:11,12). The Gospel is the truth of God expressed in and through the Son. To reject the Son and the Gospel declared by Him is to call God a liar:

"He that believeth on the Son of God hath the witness in himself: he that believeth not God hath made Him a liar; because he believeth not the record that God gave of His Son" (I John 5:10). Men deny the Word — they did in the days of Jesus, and they will until He comes again; but in spite of what man may say or think about the Word, the Triune Witness is in heaven. The eternal Word is forever settled in heaven.

Jesus, THE WORD, is in heaven now, seated at the right hand of God the Father (Heb. 1:3). The fact that Jesus is there, seated at God's right hand, declares three things:

A. His hands are scarred, testifying that He was nailed to the cross and lifted up as declared in John 3:14,15.

B. The sacrifice of His blood has been accepted, because God has exalted Him and given Him a name that is above every name. God has appointed Him the High Priest forever, to make intercession for believers (I Tim. 2:5; I John 2:1,2).

C. The fact that Jesus is seated at the right hand of God the Father declares that His ministry on earth was finished, accepted by God, and He is the One—the *only* one—who is able to confess us to the Father and mediate between us and the Father. His life, death, burial and resurrection were a divine success; and the fact that He is now seated at the right hand of God the Father testifies that God acknowledges the completeness of the finished work of the Son of His love.

The death of Jesus was NOT in vain. Sinners ARE saved by believing in His finished work. Believers ARE sustained and kept by confessing to Jesus the Mediator our shortcomings and our spiritual needs. Therefore, the Word that came down from heaven, from outer space, to declare God, DID declare God, finished the work God sent Him to do, returned and has been accepted by God, and is now seated at the right hand of God; but the same Word will return again from outer space to this earth.

III.

One day the peoples of this earth will stand speechless and aghast as they gaze into the heavens and see what is recorded in Revelation 19 by John the Beloved, who said, "In the beginning was the Word, and the Word was WITH God, and the Word WAS God." It was John who said, "There are three that bear record in heaven: The Father, the Word, and the Holy Ghost. And these three are one." The same beloved disciple declares:

"And I saw heaven opened, and behold a white horse; and He that sat upon him was called Faithful and True, and in righteousness He doth judge and make war. His eyes were as a flame of fire, and on His head were many crowns; and He had a name written, that no man knew, but He Himself. And He was clothed with a vesture dipped in blood: and His name is called The Word of God.

"And the armies which were in heaven followed Him upon white horses, clothed in fine linen, white and clean. And out of His mouth goeth a sharp sword, that with it He should smite the nations: and He shall rule them with a rod of iron: and He treadeth the winepress of the fierceness and wrath of Almighty God. And He hath on His vesture and on His thigh a name written, KING OF KINGS, AND LORD OF LORDS" (Rev. 19:11—16).

In the past, God has allowed man to go only so far, and then called him to halt. This was true in Noah's day. It was true in Nimrod's day when man imagined to build a tower to heaven. It has been true many times, and it will be true again. Today man is probing outer space. God has allowed him to go quite a distance in that direction; but I believe that before man goes much further, God will stop him! The Word will return from outer space: "AND HIS NAME IS CALLED THE WORD OF GOD." Thus the name of the Rider of the beautiful white horse. who leads multi-millions of white horses and their riders. Jesus, THE WORD, is the leader; the saints follow on white horses.

When Jesus appears in the sky, riding a beautiful white horse, His appearing will declare three things:

A.   God is saying "Amen" to the message of the Gospel.

The garment testifies to this. Without the shedding of blood there is no remission: *"He was clothed with a vesture dipped in blood."* Men must believe in the blood or they will suffer the shedding of their own blood in tragic judgment.

B.   Christ's appearing is God's "Amen" to His greatness in heaven: *"The armies which were in heaven followed Him upon white horses."* Jesus is the leader, the One altogether lovely, the fairest of ten thousand, the "Alpha, the Omega, the beginning and the ending" (Rev. 1:8).

C.   His appearing on the white horse points to the righteousness of God: *"Out of His mouth goeth a sharp sword, that with it He should smite the nations."* Jesus is not only the Word — He is *the Rock*. Those who fall upon the Rock are broken; but those upon whom the Rock falls will be ground into powder!

The return of the Word from outer space will be glorious to many, but to others it will be disastrous, tragic,

168

and judgment beyond man's description. Yes, out of His mouth goeth a sharp sword—*the Word*, quick, powerful, and sharper than any two-edged sword; and it is with the Word that He will smite the nations. Jesus does not need atomic bombs, guided missiles, and supersonic jets — He needs only the Word.

When the Word first came from outer space, the love of God was announced, the gift of God was announced, the proposition of God ("whosoever will") was announced. Jesus said, "Verily, verily, I say unto you, He that heareth MY WORD, and believeth on Him that sent me, hath everlasting life, and shall not come into condemnation; but is passed from death unto life" (John 5:24). We are saved by God's grace, and God's grace becomes ours by faith. The only way man can obtain faith is by hearing the Word (Rom. 10:17).

When the Word next appears from outer space, the Word will announce judgment — such judgment as man has never known or witnessed upon the face of this earth. In Revelation 6 we are clearly told that men will beg the rocks and mountains to fall on them. Kings and great men, chief captains, will pray for the rocks to fall on them and hide them "from the face of Him that sitteth upon the throne and from the wrath of the Lamb."

It is further declared that men will be covered with running sores. The seas will turn to blood. The fountains of fresh water will be changed to blood, and men will be given blood to drink. The sun will scorch men with heat and they will "gnaw their tongues for pain!" (Rev. 16).

If we hear the Word, we will be saved. But if we refuse to hear the Word, "WE MAKE GOD A LIAR!" (I John 5:10). Therefore we must suffer the consequences—judgment in the lake of fire that burns with brimstone, where the beast and false prophet are, and all who reject the Word will be tormented with fire and brimstone forever and forever! (Rev. 20:10,15).

Hear the Word. Receive the Word — and be saved!

THE YOUNG MAN WITH AN MMM DEGREE

THE YOUNG MAN WITH AN MMM DEGREE

"And when He (Jesus) was gone forth into the way, there came one running, and kneeled to Him, and asked Him, Good Master, what shall I do that I may inherit eternal life?

"And Jesus said unto him, Why callest thou me good? There is none good but one, that is, God. Thou knowest the commandments, Do not commit adultery, Do not kill, Do not steal, Do not bear false witness, Defraud not, Honour thy father and mother.

"And he answered and said unto Him, Master, all these have I observed from my youth. Then Jesus beholding him loved him, and said unto him, One thing thou lackest: go thy way, sell whatsoever thou hast, and give to the poor, and thou shalt have treasure in heaven: and come, take up the cross, and follow me.

"And he was sad at that saying, and went away grieved: for he had great possessions" (Mark 10:17–22).

The young man in our Scripture would be welcomed into almost any church today. He could be chairman of the board of deacons, he could be Sunday school superintendent, he could be whatever he wanted to be, no questions asked. He had three excellent qualifications: Manners, Morals, and Money — and these are things that count heavily today. This young man would make a good "joiner," but not much of a disciple. Salvation is free, but discipleship can be costly!

Jesus invited those who followed Him to take up the cross. One of His disciples said, "Lord, suffer me first to go and bury my father." But Jesus replied, *"Follow me — and let the dead bury their dead"* (Matt. 8:21,22).

On another occasion, one said, "Lord, I will follow thee; but let me first go bid them farewell, which are at

173

home at my house." Jesus replied, *"No man, having put his hand to the plough, and looking back, is fit for the kingdom of God"* (Luke 9:61,62).

Speaking to the twelve men whom He had chosen, He said, "Think not that I am come to send peace on earth: I came not to send peace, but a sword. For I am come to set a man at variance against his father, and the daughter against her mother, and the daughter in law against her mother in law. And a man's foes shall be they of his own household. *He that loveth father or mother more than me is not worthy of me: and he that loveth son or daughter more than me is not worthy of me. And he that taketh not his cross, and followeth after me, is not worthy of me"* (Matt. 10:34—38).

Instead of a life of popularity and plenty, Jesus promised His disciples poverty and persecution. He said, "Foxes have holes, and birds of the air have nests; but the Son of man hath not where to lay His head" (Luke 9:58). In Matthew 10:16—22 He said, "Behold, I send you forth as sheep in the midst of wolves . . . for they will deliver you up to the councils, and they will scourge you in their synagogues; and ye shall be brought before governors and kings for my sake . . . *and ye shall be hated of all men for my name's sake . . . .*"

So, to the young man in our Scripture text He said, *"SELL ALL, and come, follow me!"* The liberals and the modernists would have said, "Use milder terms. Don't drive the young man away with harsh demands and dogmatic stipulations. Lead him gently into the church, get him to join — *and then lead him into full surrender!*"

Those are the tactics of the devil. With Jesus, one does not gradually "let go." It is all or nothing with Him. And you will notice that when the young man went away sorrowfully, Jesus did not call him back and modify His terms. *Man* has softened the terms of salvation, but GOD has made no changes. Man says, "Join." Jesus says, "Ye must be *born from above!*" Man preaches, "Turn over a new leaf," but Jesus demands a new creation (II Cor. 5:17). Liberals invite men to line up with the church of their choice. Jesus invites, "Come unto me, all ye that labour and are heavy laden, and I will give you rest" (Matt. 11:28).

As I have previously stated, most churches would have considered this rich young man an excellent candidate for membership because outwardly he was well qualified—with manners, morals, and money.

His Manners

"*. . . There came one running, and kneeled to Him.*" This young man met Jesus in the right manner, in humility; he did not approach Him in a haughty, proud spirit as did the Pharisees and scribes. He knelt at the feet of Jesus, and certainly we must commend him for his mannerly approach to the Master. Every sinner seeking salvation should meet Jesus on bended knee insofar as attitude is concerned. It is not necessary to bow upon one's knees in order to be saved, but such an act does denote humility and respect for the sinless Son of God.

The young man "came *running.*" He was in dead earnest. And when he spoke to Jesus he addressed Him as "*good Master.*" Those words sound good to the average person. Was not Jesus "good"? He was a good Man, was He not? Indeed, He *was* good — but He was more than that: *He was God in flesh!* (II Cor. 5:19). He looked down into the upturned face of this remarkable young man and asked, "Why callest thou me good? There is none good but one, that is, God."

Was Jesus unnecessarily harsh and unkind? Should He have answered in a different way? He knew the heart

175

of the young man kneeling at His feet, just as He knows men's hearts today (John 2:25); and He knew that this young man was approaching Him as a *teacher*, not as the Son of God. Therefore He said, in essence, "If I am *good*, then I am God. And if I am NOT GOD, then I am not *good*."

Like many today, this young man was willing and ready to accept Jesus as a good man and a great teacher, one who set a very good example that should be followed; but to receive Him as God, *very God in flesh*, NEVER! According to his judgment, Jesus was divine only as WE are divine, and this is what the liberals and modernists of today say about Him.

But to be born again, to "inherit eternal life" as the rich young man wanted to do, we must receive Him as very God—begotten by the Holy Ghost, born of a virgin—the beloved, only Son of God who died on a cross for our sin. If we refuse to believe on Him as such, then our destiny is an eternity in hell!

If Jesus was "good," then He was God in flesh — otherwise He was the world's greatest and vilest imposter. He claimed to be God's Son, He claimed equality with the Father. He said, "I and my Father are ONE." If He was NOT conceived of the Holy Ghost and born of the virgin Mary, if He was not actually the only begotten SON OF GOD, then He was conceived out of wedlock and born of a harlot, for Mary was not married to Joseph, she was only betrothed to him, when she was found to be with child:

"Now the birth of Jesus Christ was on this wise: When as His mother Mary was espoused to Joseph, before they came together, she was found with child of the Holy Ghost. Then Joseph her husband, being a just man, and not willing to make her a publick example, was minded to put her away privily. But while he thought on these things, behold, the angel of the Lord appeared unto him in a

176

dream, saying, Joseph, thou son of David, fear not to take unto thee Mary thy wife: for that which is conceived in her is of the Holy Ghost. And she shall bring forth a son, and thou shalt call His name JESUS: for He shall save His people from their sins" (Matt. 1:18—21).

Thus, we can easily see that Jesus must necessarily be the very Son of God, or else He was an imposter. He was either the *best* or the *worst* this world has ever known. We know that it has been proved that He was the very best, for the words He spoke and the miracles He performed were verified by God's audible acknowledgement, "This is my beloved Son, in whom I am well pleased. Hear ye HIM!"

But the rich young ruler did not *believe* that Jesus was the Son of God. Why do I say this? It is proved by God's infallible Word:

"Whosoever believeth that Jesus is the Christ is born of God . . ." (I John 5:1).

"Verily, verily, I say unto you, He that heareth my Word, and believeth on Him that sent me, hath everlasting life, and shall not come into condemnation; but is passed from death unto life" (John 5:24).

This young man ran to Jesus, fell at His feet, and asked, "What must I do to inherit eternal life?" Jesus answered Him — and he heard the words. But he did not believe what he heard. He met the Christ of God, but he refused to receive Him as the very SON of God. Every word Jesus spoke was the Word of God, but concerning this young man we read, *"He was sad at that saying, and went away grieved . . . ."*

He refused to believe the Word of God. He did not depart *rejoicing*, believing on the Lord Jesus Christ as his personal Saviour. If he HAD believed, he would have gladly followed Him, as did blind Bartimaeus and others.

Men who believe on the Lord Jesus as Saviour will automatically follow Him.

This rich young man had manners that were impeccable — but his faith was zero.

His Morals

Notice the words of Jesus: *"Thou knowest the commandments . . . ."* He did not ask this young man IF he knew the commandments, and from this amazing circumstance the rich young ruler should have realized the fact that he was in the presence of a very extraordinary Person.

Jesus then named six of the commandments — and it is significant that the commandments He enumerated are those that have to do with man's relationship to and dealings with his fellowman. He said, "Do not commit adultery. . . Do not kill. . . Do not steal. . . Do not bear false witness. . . Do not defraud. . . Honor thy father and thy mother."

Why did not Jesus name the *first* commandment, which says, "Thou shalt have no other gods before Me"? (Ex. 20:3). He knew that this young man had another god, an interest that was usurping God's rightful place in his heart; and He therefore named only those commandments which He knew were possible for man to keep.

The rich young ruler replied, "Master, *all these have I observed from my youth*" — and Jesus did not deny the truth of his statement! It is altogether possible—though not probable—that the young man HAD kept the six commandments named; and if so, then his morals were certainly far above average. If he had kept those commandments then he was not guilty of adultery, he was not guilty of murder, he was not guilty of the ugly sin of bearing false witness against others (and most of us, at one time or another *have* been guilty of this). He would not have been guilty of cheating, and he would have had honor and devotion toward his parents. In other words, if he had kept all six of these commandments, he was a model boy—clean, honest, upright, without fault or blemish insofar as morals were concerned.

Good morals are commendable — but they will not save us from hell, nor even help to save us. Only the blood of Jesus makes us fit for heaven. It is possible to be morally clean—and yet be hopelessly lost!

Luke 18:9—14 tells of two men who went into the temple to pray. One of them told the Lord how good he was, how clean he lived, how thankful he was that he was not like other men — but *that man* went home without salvation. The second man in this passage of Scripture came before God in prayer, too humble to lift his eyes to heaven. Instead, he prayed, "God, be merciful to me a sinner"—and that man went home saved and satisfied!

During my years in evangelistic work I have had many people say to me, "Brother Greene, I live the very best I know how, I pay my honest debts, I treat my family right, I attend church regularly and pay liberally to support its work. I do my very best to live by the Golden Rule. What *more* can I do?" To this question I always answer, "You must be BORN AGAIN!" Without the new birth, man cannot see the kingdom of God (John 3:3).

We have found the rich young ruler's manners to be above average and his morals to be without blemish — yet Jesus said to him, *"ONE THING thou lackest."*

His Money

". . . Jesus beholding him *loved him*, and said unto him, One thing thou lackest: Go thy way, sell whatsoever thou hast, and give to the poor, and thou shalt have treasure in heaven: *and come*, TAKE UP THE CROSS, AND FOLLOW ME."

But the young man did not attempt to answer. He

179

turned and went away, sad of countenance and deeply grieved, *"for he had great possessions."*

"So," you say, "his money damned him!" No, his money did NOT damn him. He was damned by the same sin that has sent every other soul to hell that has ever gone there—the sin of unbelief. He rejected Jesus. He refused to hear the Word which would have brought saving faith to his poor, hungry heart (Rom. 10:17).

Jesus told him plainly to sell his great possessions, give the money to the poor, and he would have treasure in heaven — but he refused to do so. He loved his wealth—a fact proved by his refusal to surrender it to Jesus. He was invited to take up a cross and walk with the Saviour—a life of traveling, with all expenses paid, so to speak. Jesus offered to relieve him of the care and anxiety imposed upon him by his vast riches — but he refused the offer. He was willing to keep the commandments, he was willing to do almost anything to be saved — but when it came to giving up his wealth and following Jesus, he went away sorrowing, turning his back upon salvation and upon the treasure promised him in heaven.

The simple truth of the matter is that this young man simply did not believe Jesus! He was not willing to trust the Lord to handle his business for him. He came to the Master Teacher to find out what he could do in order to get to heaven — but he did not expect his possessions to be involved. If he had believed what Jesus said, if he had believed that Jesus was able to do what He promised, he would immediately have sold all that he had and followed Him. But he did not believe.

The sin of unbelief has damned every soul who burns in hell today, and the same sin will damn those who go to hell from now until Jesus comes! The young man's money did not damn him, oh no! His damnation was his failure

180

to trust Jesus and take Him at His Word — and this same unbelief will also send YOU to hell if you do not trust Jesus and believe His Word. If you are not saved, dear reader, God grant this be the moment you trust Him for salvation!

"He that believeth on HIM is not condemned: but he that believeth NOT is condemned ALREADY, because he hath not believed in the name of the only begotten Son of God" (John 3:18).

In John 12:48 Jesus said, "He that rejecteth me, and receiveth not my words, hath one that judgeth him: *the Word that I have spoken, the same shall judge him in the last day."*

The young man was saddened by the Lord's reply to his question, and he went away grieved. What a tragedy! Who would have thought it? He seemed so sincere, so earnest — and he was such a humble young man. Everybody said he was one of the finest fellows they had ever met. It is hard indeed to believe that such a fine, stalwart, clean, upright, honest, and mannerly young man would go to hell — but he did! We have no record that he ever again came to Jesus, and I believe that had this boy ever been saved, God would have told us about it!

Good, honest, upright, sincere folk go to hell — but wait a minute! SAVED people do NOT go to hell. We are not saved because we have good manners, good morals, or lots of money. We are saved by trusting Jesus with our all—all that we are and all that we have—for time and for eternity.

"Trust and obey, for there's no other way
To be happy in Jesus, but to trust and obey!"

What about it, dear reader? Are you trusting in your good manners, your good morals, your good deeds, or good use of your money to get you into heaven when you die?

If you are, there is a big disappointment in store for you. There is only ONE WAY to heaven: Jesus said, "I am the WAY, the TRUTH, and the LIFE: NO MAN cometh unto the Father, but by ME" (John 14:6).

Many people, like the rich young ruler, live the very best they know how, give sacrificially of what they possess, and accomplish all the good they possibly can — but they still lack ONE THING: they lack trust in Jesus as their personal Saviour. If you hope to enter heaven, then take God's Word for the fact that Jesus is the DOOR—the *only* door—by which you can enter there (John 10:9). Jesus is the water of life (John 4:14). He is the bread of life (John 6:48). No man can come to God except through HIM.

The Philippian jailer asked, "What must I do to be saved?" Paul and Silas replied, "Believe on the Lord Jesus Christ, and thou shalt be saved, and thy house" (Acts 16:31).

If you are not saved, dear reader, then believe on the Lord Jesus this moment and He will save your soul. You may ask, "*What does it mean* to believe on Jesus?" To believe on the Lord Jesus Christ unto salvation is simply to believe that He is the only begotten Son of God, that He died to save you, that He is able and willing to save you, and that He WILL save you if you will only take Him at His word. Trust your soul, spirit, and body into His hands, and believe in simple, childlike faith that He is able to do for you what you could not do for yourself.

Whatever God demands, He provides. Whatever is required of us in order to enter heaven, He has already provided in His only begotten Son. Good manners will not make us fit for heaven. Morals that are above reproach do not make us fit for heaven. Money will buy a lot of nice things . . . money "talks" on earth, but it is dumb at the judgment bar of God! What is money to God? *HE paves*

182

streets with pure gold! We are not redeemed with silver and gold, "but with the precious blood of Christ, as of a lamb without blemish and without spot" (I Pet. 1:18,19).

Christ's blood has been shed for the remission of sins (Matt. 26:28).

It is not God's will that any should perish, but that all come to repentance (II Pet. 3:9).

Christ's invitation is to all — not one is excluded: "Come unto me . . . and I will give you rest" (Matt. 11:28–30).

His promise is, *"Him that cometh to me I will in no wise cast out"* (John 6:37).

Sinner friend, if you die in your sin and drop into the pits of the damned to burn forever in the lake of fire, it will be of your choosing, and not because God so willed it!

Jesus loved the rich young ruler — the Scripture plainly tells us so. He tenderly invited him to lay aside treasures of the world and follow Him, but of his own free will the young man turned and walked away. What will YOU do? Will you lay this message aside and forget it? Or will you recognize your lost condition and trust Jesus as your Saviour? If you are unsaved, you MUST do one or the other. You cannot ignore this invitation to be saved and expect to remain the same. After having read this message, you will either have a softer heart, or you will have a heart hardened and less receptive to the call of God on future invitations.

Christian, bow your head and thank God that you are saved — and then pray for those who, as yet, do not know Christ as Saviour!

"WHOSE SOEVER SINS YE REMIT"

"WHOSE SOEVER SINS YE REMIT"

"Whose soever sins ye remit, they are remitted unto them; and whose soever sins ye retain, they are retained" *(John 20:23).*

To many, this is one of the most confusing verses in the Bible; but when we study and rightly divide the Word of Truth, it becomes as plain as John 3:16.

Roman Catholics teach that Christ conferred upon the Roman priests the authority to grant absolution (forgiveness) of sins. Many poor souls have been deceived by this teaching, while many others have wondered just what the verse does mean. If you will forget all you have heard and read, forget what men have said, by the grace of God and through His Word we will learn the true meaning of this verse of Scripture. *"Come now, and let us reason together."*

Paul tells us in I Corinthians 10:32, "Give none offence, neither to the Jews, nor to the Gentiles, nor to the church of God." When studying the Word of God we must always consider to whom the words of the Scripture were spoken, and also the time element which applies to that passage. For example: God told Noah to build an ark — *but He does not want us to build an ark today.* God told Abraham to take his son Isaac up into the mountain and offer him as a sacrifice — but God does not want me to put my boy on an altar and lift a knife to slay him. Yet in all these glorious passages are wonderful truths for us in this day of Grace!

In our present text, let us consider, first: *To whom did the Lord Jesus speak these words?* Secondly: *Consider the time* when the words were spoken. From the context in which we find this verse, we know the words were spoken either to the disciples in general, or to the apostles in particular.

If Jesus spoke these words to the disciples in general, then this passage cannot possibly signify that some special power is conferred upon any special group. If the words were spoken to disciples in general, then ALL disciples would have the power to remit (or forgive) sin! In that case, the Roman priests have no right to claim that power to forgive sins has been conferred upon *them*. The Romanist priest-class did not come into existence until many years after Jesus spoke the words of our text.

On the other hand, if the words were spoken to the apostles in particular, the Roman teaching is just as far out of line, because there is no place in the Gospels where the apostles are called priests! The apostles of our Lord Jesus were plain, ordinary working men whom the Lord called to follow Him. They left their nets and fishing boats, their tax-collector's table, whatever profession they followed, and gave their time and talents to the Lord Jesus in humble service and preaching of the Word. The apostles were never ordained priests, they never claimed to be priests, and nowhere in the Scripture were they ever *called* priests.

In the New Testament Church *all believers* are priests. Read I Peter 2:5–9 and Revelation 1:6. From these passages you will learn that in this day of Grace, all believers are "a royal priesthood."

The church of Rome claims that her priesthood is derived from the apostles of the Lord Jesus, and that the authority to absolve from sin is transmitted by apostolic succession! If you will study church history and Bible

188

antiquity, however, you will find great *historical gaps* in that supposed succession. No person on earth, including Roman priests, have Bible grounds upon which to claim the right to absolve from sin, nor to confess the sinner: "For there is one God, and *one Mediator between God and men, the man Christ Jesus*" (I Tim. 2:5).

What about the time element involved in our text? When did the Lord Jesus speak these words? If you will study the context of the passage, you will find that these words of our Lord were spoken before the Church had come into existence. The Church is not mentioned at all in either the preceding or the following Scriptures. The words of our text do not refer to the Church, nor do they have anything to do with the Church age. *These words have to do with the Kingdom of Heaven.*

One of the major errors of the church of Rome is that of confusing *the Church* and *the Kingdom of Heaven*. Many Protestant ministers also confuse the two by making them one and the same.

The church of Rome claims that Jesus gave Peter the keys to the Church in Matthew 16:19. Jesus did no such thing! He said to Peter, "I will give unto thee *the keys of the kingdom of heaven*." The words of our text refer to the Kingdom of Heaven—not to the Church, the body of Christ (Eph. 5:22–32; Col. 1:18,24). When these words were spoken by our Lord, the Church was yet future, and after it did come into existence at Pentecost the keys were never mentioned again.

If this Scripture refers to the Church, to the doctrines of the Church, or if it should be applied to the ministers of the Church, why is this not written into the Epistles which were given specifically TO the Church? The *Pastoral Epistles* (I Timothy through Philemon) do not one

189

time suggest that ministers have the power or authority to remit sin. The *Church Epistles* (Romans through II Thessalonians) do not once mention ministers having authority to absolve from sin—nor to confess the sinner. There is absolutely no mention of a priest-class in God's instructions to the New Testament Church . . . not one mention of an apostle claiming the right to absolve from sin. Read all the Epistles — and you will not find one suggestion of such doctrine.

What do we mean when we say the words of our text concern the *Kingdom of Heaven*? Multitudes of church people know nothing of the difference between: (1) The Church, (2) The Kingdom of Heaven, and (3) The Kingdom of God. I do not have time and space to discuss these subjects fully in this message, but I will give a brief outline:

The *Kingdom of Heaven* will be right here upon this earth (Matt. 6:10). Jesus will sit on the throne of David in Jerusalem and reign here upon this earth for one thousand years (Rev. 20:6; Isaiah 9:6,7; Isaiah 11).

The *Kingdom of God* is a spiritual kingdom within the believer (Rom. 14:17). The Kingdom of God is universal, including angels (Luke 13:28,29; Heb. 12:22,23). The Kingdom of God is entered only by the new birth (John 3:3–5). The Kingdom of God comes not with outward show (Luke 17:20).

The *Church* is the body of Christ, made up of all born again believers (Eph. 5:21–33). The Church differs from the Kingdom of Heaven and from the Kingdom of God; we should never confuse the three. Jesus is the head of the Church; He will be the King in the Kingdom of Heaven when it is set up here on earth. We must "rightly divide the Word of Truth" if we are ever to understand the Bible

The primary subject of the preaching of the Lord Jesus was the offer of the Kingdom of Heaven to God's chosen people, Israel. His message was rejected by Israel and they crucified their King! They asked for Barabbas, the robber, instead of their King; and they have been robbed ever since.

During the period covered by the book of Acts, the Jews were given a renewed opportunity to receive their Messiah-King. The approximately thirty years covered by Acts was a suspense period. The nation Israel was given a chance to repent; the signs at Pentecost (and other miraculous signs) testified that they had crucified their Messiah. But they rejected the message of the apostles just as they had rejected the message of their Lord. The signs recorded in the book of Acts testify that God did give Israel another opportunity to receive her King; but after they refused to hear—even though the messages were accompanied by signs and wonders which proved them to be from God—God then withdrew the signs. As Israel refused again and again to hear the message of her King, God opened the mystery of the Church that had been hidden from the beginning (Eph. 3:3–10).

The apostles of Jesus Christ were a group of men in a category all to themselves. They were specially endowed with miraculous gifts and supernatural prerogatives for a special ministry at a special time. There have been no other apostles since the apostles of Jesus passed from the scene of action. Those men had power and authority no other men have ever had, and when they completed their ministry they went on to be with their Lord. *Nowhere in the Word of God can you find a suggestion that the apostles were to have successors!*

There are no apostles in this day of Grace: "And

He gave some, apostles; and some, prophets; and some, evangelists; and some, pastors and teachers'' (Eph. 4:11). The apostles and prophets are all dead and gone on to rest with Jesus; their ministry is finished on earth. The prophecy has been given, the apostles have completed their work, and God is now operating through evangelists, pastors and teachers.

In reading the context for our present text, we find that Jesus appeared to the disciples in the upper room (behind closed doors for fear of the Jews). He stepped into their midst and said, "Peace be unto you." He then showed them His hands and His feet, and they recognized Him as their Lord. Jesus again said unto them, "Peace be unto you," and then added, "As my Father hath sent me, even so send I you. And when He had said this, He breathed on them, and saith unto them, Receive ye the Holy Ghost: Whose soever sins ye remit, they are remitted unto them; and whose soever sins ye retain, they are retained."

The power to remit or retain sins was given to the apostles in conjunction with a special endowment of the Holy Ghost, to carry on the work which Jesus had begun, but which had come to a sudden climax when He was crucified. The statement had nothing to do with setting up the apostles as priests to forgive sins, nor to confess people to the Father. Jesus was crucified . . . He was cut off (Isa. 53:8); but His ministry must continue. The apostles were appointed to carry on that ministry until the Church was fully revealed. They had power to heal all kinds of diseases, they could raise the dead — they had *unlimited* power; but I challenge anyone to find one place in Scripture where any apostle claimed that he was able to forgive the sinner and save a lost soul!

On the day of Pentecost, when the multitudes cried

192

out, "Men and brethren, what shall we do?" what did Peter tell them? Did he tell them to come to his office and confess their sins, and that he would then absolve those sins? Did he tell that great host of souls to come to the apostles and receive remission for sin? HE DID NOT!

In Acts 2:38 Peter preached the same Gospel Jesus preached, the same Gospel John the Baptist preached: "Repent! Repent!!" Yes, Peter preached repentance in the name of Jesus Christ for remission of sin. If Peter was the first pope, if the apostles were the first priests, why did they not set up a confessional and confess the people who wanted forgiveness of sins? They knew that *God alone could forgive sins*, and that *Jesus alone could confess the sinner to the Father* (I Tim. 2:5).

The apostles to whom Jesus spoke the words of our text not once advertised themselves as priests. They went out preaching the Gospel of the Grace of God, telling poor lost sinners to repent in the name of Jesus for the remission of sins. No, dearly beloved, the words of our text do not give priests authority to absolve sins, nor authority to confess the sinner to the heavenly Father. There is ONLY ONE who has that authority — and He won that authority through the blood of His cross: ". . . Who . . . when He had by Himself purged our sins, sat down on the right hand of the Majesty on high" (Heb. 1:3). God's Word says:

"There is one God, *and one Mediator between God and men*, the man, CHRIST JESUS." Any man who sets himself up as a priest of God with the authority to forgive sins is a minister of the devil! Be not deceived, dear soul— Jesus alone can forgive your sins, and when HE FORGIVES your sins, *they are gone forever*!

When you believe on Jesus as your personal Saviour, *you are a priest and a king*! (I Peter 2:9). Do not be led about by cults and "isms" of this apostate age. Follow Jesus, read His Word, live by the Bible—and you will be in that number when the saints go marching in. "If we confess our sins (to God), He is faithful and just to forgive us our sins, and to cleanse us from all unrighteousness" (I John 1:9).

NO SHORT CUT

NO SHORT CUT

"Thomas saith unto Him, Lord, we know not whither thou goest; and how can we know the way? Jesus saith unto him, I am the way, the truth, and the life: no man cometh unto the Father, but by me" (John 14:5,6).

The Lord Jesus Christ came into the world for one primary purpose: He came to save the lost: "For the Son of man is come to seek and to save that which was lost" (Luke 19:10).

Christ had no illusions as to what His mission meant. From the very beginning His eye was singled on Calvary — He knew He had come into the world to die. Yet Satan unfolded before the eyes of Jesus a plan which he said would solve all the problems of evangelism:

"Again, the devil taketh Him up into an exceeding high mountain, and sheweth Him all the kingdoms of the world, and the glory of them; and saith unto Him, All these things will I give thee, if thou wilt fall down and worship me. Then saith Jesus unto him, Get thee hence, Satan: for it is written, Thou shalt worship the Lord thy God, and Him only shalt thou serve" (Matt. 4:8—10).

It is my belief that *the entire world* was spread before the eyes of the Saviour at that time. I believe He saw India, China, Japan, Russia, the British Isles, the huge continent of Africa, the United States of America and the great cities of western civilization. He saw every island in the sea. *He saw it all* — and realized that in all these places Satan would resist Him, resist His love, His eternal purpose; and would do all in his diabolical power to damn every soul wheresoever souls were found.

197

Jesus *saw* this mighty conflict, and He knew it would be bloody, bitter, and long. He knew that it would continue down through the centuries, and that rivers of blood would flow as a result of the warfare between Himself and the prince of this world. He also knew that in the battle, even though final victory would be His, many souls would pass into eternity to spend the endless ages in the lake of fire. It was against this forbidding background that Satan made his insidious offer to the Son of God.

Someone may be saying, *"But these kingdoms were not Satan's to give."* If that is your thought, beloved, I refer you to Luke 4:5—7: "And the devil, taking Him up into an high mountain, shewed unto Him all the kingdoms of the world *in a moment of time.* And the devil said unto Him, All this power will I give thee, and the glory of them: *FOR THAT IS DELIVERED UNTO ME; and to whomsoever I will I give it.* If thou therefore wilt worship me, all shall be thine."

My dear friend, according to God's infallible Word these kingdoms *were* Satan's to give to whomsoever he would! Do you see Jesus as He stands in the presence of a very personal devil? I do not believe Satan came to the Son of God in the guise of a roaring lion — I believe he stood as an angel of light; and he placed before the Saviour all the peoples of all the world, and Jesus saw them all "in a moment of time." Satan said, "Fall down and worship me, and I will give all these to thee." But for the Lord Jesus Christ there was no short cut. He was man — but He was God. He was the God-Man, and He came into the world to do the will of the Father.

You will notice that Christ did not challenge Satan's ability to do what he promised. If we study the suggestion made by Satan we will see that the offer contained his promise to withdraw all Satanic opposition — there would be no more surging passions of temptation, suggestions of wickedness, godlessness, and vice — IF Jesus would fall down and worship him!

Consider what this would mean. If Satan withdrew his opposition in Africa, Asia, China, these millions of peoples would be delivered from superstition and shame. The underworld gangs of the great cities would become gentlemen overnight, and the entire world would be released from Satan's power. The shackles of sin would be broken, and the power of *death as a result of sin* would be destroyed.

"All this will I give thee" — but the promise carried with it Satan's *"IF."* Considered in the light of human wisdom and reasoning, the offer was most attractive and inviting; it would be foolish to turn it down. But Jesus entertained no idea of accepting. He refused the offer immediately — and by so doing made it clear that He considered the integrity of His own soul to be of far more importance than winning earth's millions in a moment of time. Thus He teaches that the end does NOT justify the means if the means is to destroy the sanctity and integrity of the soul.

Jesus was (and is) the Truth. Satan was (and is) the Lie. The only place I have found in the Bible where Satan ever told the truth was in his conversation with Eve — and even then, in telling the truth, *he lied.* He said to Eve, "God doth know that in the day ye eat thereof, then your eyes shall be opened, and ye shall be as gods, knowing good and evil" (Gen. 3:5).

Eve believed what Satan said. She ate, she gave to Adam and HE ate, *and their eyes WERE opened* — but what Satan did not make clear was that they would not become as the *true God*, but as the god of this age—Satan himself —

and that is exactly what happened.

Yes, the father of lies, even in telling the truth on one occasion, told only a half-truth because a lie was contained in his statement — a lie concealing from Adam and Eve the fact that when their eyes were opened they would see the shame of their nakedness, and would fear the voice of God — a voice which, up to that time, had brought them comfort, joy, and blessed fellowship.

Satan offers many attractive rewards — but they are all prefaced with "IF" — and those "if's" are prelude to sadness, sorrow, heartbreak, disappointment, and disaster.

Victory In Jesus

The account of the temptation of Jesus is found in Matthew 4:1–11 and Luke 4:1–13.   Satan hurled at Him every temptation hell affords.

He first tempted Him through the *lust of the flesh:* "If thou be the Son of God, command this stone that it be made bread."

He tempted Him through the *pride of life* by taking Him into the Holy City and setting Him on a pinnacle of the temple, and saying, "Cast thyself down from hence: For it is written, He shall give His angels charge over thee, to keep thee: And in their hands they shall bear thee up, lest at any time thou dash thy foot against a stone."   But Jesus replied, "Thou shalt not tempt the Lord thy God."

Then — Satan's last insidious offer, made through the *lust of the eye* as he showed Jesus all the kingdoms of the world and promised to give them to Him if He would only fall down and worship him.

John tells us that "all that is in the world, the lust of the flesh, and the lust of the eyes, and the pride of life, is not of the Father, but is of the world.   And the world passeth away, and the lust thereof: *but he that doeth the will of God abideth for ever*" (I John 2:15,16).

In Matthew 4:10,11 we are told that Jesus said, "Get thee hence, Satan: for it is written, Thou shalt worship the Lord thy God, and Him only shalt thou serve. Then the devil leaveth Him, and, behold, *angels came and ministered unto Him.*"

Though tempted in all points as we are, Christ was without sin (Heb. 4:15). He conquered the world, the flesh, the devil, death, hell, and the grave — and *WE are more than conquerors through Him*!

After His victory over the devil, "Jesus returned in the power of the Spirit into Galilee: and there went out a fame of Him through all the region round about. And He taught in their synagogues, being glorified of all" (Luke 4:14,15).

"AND FROM THAT TIME, JESUS BEGAN TO PREACH, AND TO SAY, REPENT . . ." (Matt. 4:17).

There is no substitute for preaching, there is no substitute for repentance. The sad, sad status of the church today is that in all too many instances, what *should be* worship services have become glorified programs of entertainment instead of powerful, dynamic messages of Bible doctrine, bathed in the Holy Spirit, delivered in power, preached by men like Stephen, "full of the Holy Ghost."

When suppers, plays, and programs are substituted for the message of the Gospel, the church is on the road to suicide — and when I say *the church*, I am speaking of local assemblies, *not* the Church of the living God, against which the gates of hell cannot prevail.

A church that has more suppers and entertainments than worship services and revivals should be forced to identify itself by removing the steeple and putting a "Club" sign over the door! The Church of the living God is a *spiritual* cafeteria, where the living bread is broken and given out by Spirit-filled ministers.

"For the preaching of the cross is to them that perish foolishness; but unto us which are saved it is the power of God. For it is written, I will destroy the wisdom of the wise, and will bring to nothing the understanding of the prudent. Where is the wise? Where is the scribe? Where is the disputer of this world? Hath not God made foolish the wisdom of this world? For after that in the wisdom of God the world by wisdom knew not God, it pleased God by the foolishness of preaching to save them that believe. For the Jews require a sign, and the Greeks seek after wisdom: But we preach Christ crucified, unto the Jews a stumbling-block, and unto the Greeks foolishness; but, unto them which are called, both Jews and Greeks, Christ the power of God, and the wisdom of God. Because the foolishness of God is wiser than men; and the weakness of God is stronger than men" (I Cor. 1:18—25).

When religious leaders come to believe themselves so wise and so well educated that they know more than *God* does about how to run the church, you can mark it down that *Satan*, not the Holy Spirit, is in command. God saves sinners through the preaching of the Gospel, not through the program of denominational leaders.

"And Jesus, walking by the sea of Galilee, saw two brethren, Simon called Peter, and Andrew his brother, casting a net into the sea: for they were fishers. And He saith unto them, Follow me, and I will make you fishers of men. And they straightway left their nets, and followed Him" (Matt. 4:18—20).

God never saved a soul to sit and take it easy while others are madly rushing into a Christless eternity. Here were two new converts — babes in Christ. They were unlearned fishermen — and yet, Jesus placed before them the prospect of catching men for God.

I believe in Christian education. I believe a call to preach is a call to study and prepare, but even a babe in Christ can give testimony to the saving grace of God. Jesus converted, called, and commissioned Peter and Andrew to be fishers of men — not after a four-year course in the seminary, but immediately after conversion.

We see the effectiveness of Andrew's discipleship when food was needed for five thousand hungry men, not counting women and children. While Philip and others of the disciples were counting pennies and figuring up the number of loaves that could be bought with their scant supply, Andrew said to Jesus, "There is a lad here, which hath five barley loaves and two small fishes" (John 6:7-9).

While the others were counting the money and deciding that "it couldn't be done," Andrew was searching for bread. He found it — and even though he confessed that what he had found was very little, he knew that even that small bit, in the hands of His Lord, could be plenty! Andrew had a gift that many church members do not possess, simply because they have not completely yielded themselves to become fishers of men.

Soul-winning evangelism has been the greatest instrument, the strongest force, in the history of the New Testament Church. The Church was born in revival at Pentecost, and *it grew* in the days of revival *following* Pentecost. It has continued to grow during periods of revival under such men as Moody, Spurgeon, Luther, Billy Sunday. A church without revival and evangelism becomes a social hall, a place of entertainment, rather than a place where men are caught for Jesus in the net of the Gospel of the marvelous grace of God!

What kind of Christian are *you*? What kind of Christian am I? What kind of church are we part of? Friend, if you are not in a church that believes in evangelism and winning the lost for Jesus, you belong to a social organization, not a soul-saving station.

The Power of the Gospel

The Apostle Paul said, "I am not ashamed of the Gospel of Christ: for *it is the power of God unto salvation* to every one that believeth . . . for therein is the righteousness of God revealed . . ." (Rom. 1:16,17). Then in I Corinthians 15:1-4 Paul gives us the definition of the Gospel:

"Moreover, brethren, I declare unto you the Gospel which I preached unto you. . . For I delivered unto you first of all that which I also received, how that *Christ died* for our sins according to the Scriptures; and that *He was buried*, and that *He rose again* the third day according to the Scriptures."

Paul preached the death, burial, and resurrection of Jesus Christ, who came into this world to save sinners. He lived, He died, He was buried, He rose again, He ascended — and now He is seated at the right hand of God the Father. It has therefore pleased God to call and ordain men to preach the Gospel, and it is through the foolishness of preaching the Gospel that sinners are saved today.

In Matthew 4:23,24 we read that Jesus went about teaching, preaching, healing all manner of disease and sickness. They brought unto Him "all sick people that were taken with divers diseases and torments, and those which were possessed with devils, and those which were lunatick, and those that had the palsy; and He healed them."

Marvelous indeed! But you may say, "*Jesus* did these

204

miracles — but we are not Jesus. We are poor, finite beings." That is true. We ARE finite — but we are saved
by God's grace and indwelt by the Holy Spirit, and we have
the promise Jesus made in John 14:12: "Verily, verily, I
say unto you, He that believeth on me, the works that I do
shall he do also; *and greater works than these shall he do*;
because I go unto my Father."

What did Jesus mean by that statement? He meant
exactly what He said. During His earthly ministry, He
healed all manner of sickness and disease, performed all
manner of miracles — but these were only sidelines, they
were secondary. His primary purpose was *to seek and save
that which was lost.* He did heal — He still does. Nothing
is impossible with Him. But He did not come into the
world to heal lepers or open the eyes of the blind. He
came to open the eyes of the soul and save sinners from
their sins.

Jesus finished *His* work, and returned to the Father —
but He left with US the unfinished business of calling out
a Gentile bride for Him. When we are saved, we are indwelt by the Holy Spirit, that we might be witnesses, that
we might be fishers of men, that we might testify and
preach the Gospel of the grace of God—salvation for "whosoever will."

You and I have the Gospel, the Word of God which is
the POWER of God unto salvation. Therefore, when Jesus
said, "Greater things than these shall ye do," He was
pointing to the ministry of true servants of God who preach
the Gospel of God's grace—and through the Gospel set cap-
tives free — but notice that this is done only through the
Gospel, not through church suppers, programs, and entertainment.

Yes, there IS something greater than opening the eyes

of the physically blind. To the believers in Corinth Paul wrote, "If our Gospel be hid, it is hid to them that are lost: In whom the god of this world hath blinded the minds of them which believe not, lest *the light of the glorious Gospel of Christ* . . . should shine unto them. . . For God, who commanded the light to shine out of darkness, hath shined in our hearts, to give the light of the knowledge of the glory of God in the face of Jesus Christ" (II Cor. 4:3-6).

It would be marvelous beyond words to be able to say to a leper, "Be thou clean," and see physical leprosy depart — but there is something greater. The physical disease of leprosy kills the body, but *the leprosy of sin* destroys the soul!

In James 5:20 we read, ". . . He which converteth the sinner from the error of his way shall save a soul from death, and shall hide a multitude of sins."

Christians in this dispensation of the Church live in the most glorious age of history. We have the most glorious opportunities ever afforded mankind. Beloved, *God could have sent angels or cherubim to preach the Gospel —* but He allowed US to give out this good news of salvation!

The true Church has the message that is the only antidote for the ills of this world. We who know the Lord Jesus have the message that will cause poor, fallen men and women to be raised from the deadness of sin to newness of life in Christ Jesus.

There Are No Short Cuts

Modernism and liberalism have manufactured many short cuts today. We hear much about a social gospel, a gospel of "churchianity." Men are invited to unite with the church, live by the Golden Rule, do the best they can — but our best is not good enough. According to God's Word,

206

our best adds up to no more than filthy rags (Isaiah 64:6).

Jesus is the Door—the ONLY Door—to salvation. It *had* to be Jesus. It had to be by way of the cross — *there was no other way!* Jesus said, ". . . As Moses lifted up the serpent in the wilderness, even so MUST the Son of man be lifted up; that whosoever believeth in Him should not perish, but have eternal life" (John 3:14,15).

There is no short cut to heaven. There is no side door by which we may enter there. JESUS is the way, the truth, the life. NO MAN COMETH UNTO THE FATHER BUT BY HIM! (John 14:6).